GET OUT OF YOUR HEAD

A STUDY IN PHILIPPIANS · 6 SESSIONS

JENNIE ALLEN

Harper*Christian*
Resources

Get Out of Your Head Study
© 2020 by Jennie Allen

Published in Grand Rapids, Michigan, by HarperChristian Resources. HarperChristian Resources is a registered trademark of HarperCollins Christian Publishing, Inc.

Requests for information should be sent to customercare@harpercollins.com.

ISBN 978-0-310-17033-4 (softcover)
ISBN 978-0-310-17034-1 (ebook)

Based on the book *Get Out of Your Head* by Jennie Allen, © 2020 by Jennie Allen. Used by permission of WaterBrook Publishing, 10807 New Allegiance Drive #500, Colorado Springs, CO 80921.

HarperChristian Resources titles may be purchased in bulk for church, business, fundraising, or ministry use. For information, please e-mail ResourceSpecialist@ ChurchSource.com.

First Printing January 2020 / Printed in the United States of America

CONTENTS

WHAT DO YOU HOPE TO GET OUT OF THIS STUDY?

_____

_____

_____

_____

_____

GET HONEST

This is going to get personal, but it will be worth it. We will be dealing with the very things that make you, you. God wants to do something with those things. But until we recognize that we are made to run a race all our own, we will miss what He has for us. Be honest with yourself and honest with God. He knows all of it anyway.

ENGAGE WITH YOUR SMALL GROUP

An important part of personal growth is community. We are going to deal with the way we view God and how we are to spend our lives individually for Him. You may even need time outside of this small group to process with others your passions and gifts and purpose. Be intentional to pursue deeper conversations with others through this process.

"And you shall know the truth, and the truth shall make you free" (John 8:32 NKJV).

COMMIT TO BEING CONSISTENT AND PRESENT

Commit to being present at your group meetings, barring an emergency, and arrange your schedule so you do not miss any part in this journey. Have your lesson and projects finished when you come to the group meeting (except for this first one, of course).

GROUND RULES FOR GROUP DISCUSSION

BE CONCISE.
Share your answers to the questions while protecting others' time for sharing. Be thoughtful. Don't be afraid to share with the group, but try not to dominate the conversation.

> "Let every person be quick to hear, slow to speak" (James 1:19 ESV).

KEEP GROUP MEMBERS' STORIES CONFIDENTIAL.

Many things your group members share are things they are choosing to share with you, not with your husband or other friends. Protect each other by not allowing anything shared in the group to leave the group.

RELY ON SCRIPTURE FOR TRUTH.

We are prone to use conventional, worldly wisdom as truth. While there is value in that, this is not the place. If you feel led to respond, please only respond with God's truth and Word, not "advice."

NO COUNSELING.

Protect the group by not directing all attention on solving one person's problem. This is the place for confessing and discovery and applying truth together as a group. Your group leader will be able to direct you to more help outside the group time if you need it. Don't be afraid to ask for help.

STUDY DESIGN

In the first meeting, your groups' study guides will be passed out. Each study guide comes with free streaming access to my teaching videos. Work through the Introduction lesson together. After that, each lesson in the study guide is meant to be completed on your own during the week before coming to the group meeting. These lessons may feel different from studies you have done in the past. They are very interactive. The beginning of each lesson will involve you, your Bible, and a pen, working through Scripture and listening to God's voice. Each lesson will conclude with four projects you can do to help you further process how to live God's Word.

Don't feel as if each lesson has to be finished in one sitting; take a few blocks of time throughout the week if you need to. The goal of this study is to dig deeply into Scripture and uncover how it applies to your life, to deeply engage the mind and the heart. Projects, stories, and Bible study all play a role in it. You may be drawing or journaling or interacting with the homeless. At each group meeting you will discuss your experience in working through that week's lesson.

TERRIFIC RESOURCES FOR FURTHER PERSONAL STUDY

www.biblegateway.com

SPIRALING OUT

Work through Introduction pages 10-16 and Study pages 21-33 on your own before your next group meeting.

The first time I taught the study you're about to dive into, I gathered a room full of women in my local church to talk about what's going on in our heads. We met for six weeks, and lives were changed. The first night those women streamed into the chapel where we were meeting, they were greeted by a giant whiteboard on which was written the question, "What are you thinking about?" Attached to that board were dozens of brightly colored sticky notes with topics that might be taking up space in their thoughts, things like these:

- others' opinions
- finances
- plans

- the holidays
- the weekend
- the news

Before the women in the Bible study took their seats, they were asked to identify a few of the thoughts that were true for them and peel off those sticky notes. It was a challenging task.

Following that evening's exercise, my team and I assessed which thoughts had been taken and by how many women and which thoughts were still left on the board.

Despite dozens of positive options available on those sticky notes, guess which options got picked?

- stress at work
- stress over finances
- Am I good enough?
- Am I worthy?

- failures
- rejection
- pain

Guess which stickies remained untouched?

▶ choosing joy   ▶ good memories

▶ strength   ▶ my heart

"Hiking" did get three takers, so at least there's that.

Now, I've got to tell you, based on what these women indicated they were thinking about, I pretty much knew what assumptions they were making. Assumptions such as *If people knew how badly I'd failed, they'd never love me* and *My worth comes from my ability to be perfect. No wonder I am not worthy of much.*

As a result of those assumptions, emotions surface: frustration, anger, despondency, hopelessness, embarrassment, inadequacy, shame.

From those emotions, beliefs begin to form: *I'll never thrive in my career. I'll never be good enough. I'll never be accepted and loved. I'll never get out of debt.* We spiral down and down.

From those beliefs, actions are taken: We will numb our pain. We will hide our fear. We will fake our happiness. We will "armor up."

Those actions over time form habits, which craft the lifestyles that shape our days.

No wonder so many of us have trouble sticking to change! We fall prey to negative thinking and then wake up one day utterly defeated.

We need a new normal.

The truth is, even if our minds are a mess, Jesus offers us that new normal. It's a place where we know we're fully loved, where we're operating in our purpose, where we're running free. Our minds are strong and clear. And that's available to us as His followers—right now. But sometimes even if we know this truth, we don't believe it. And our minds spin and spin, looking to land, and yet unsure if our mind stopping is even possible. Messages get mixed and it feels like we can't quite put our feet back down on the simple truths of what it means to love Jesus and what it means to be loved by Jesus.

In these weeks together, studying the book of Philippians, we are going to remember, or perhaps discover for the first time, what it looks like to imitate Christ. What will become apparent is that the overflowing, contagious joy that comes from following the example of Jesus is directly connected to how we think.

We often don't think about the way we think. We think about the way we *feel* almost every minute. But changing the way we think seems nearly impossible. And yet the apostle Paul clearly tells us again and again—conforming our minds to Christ is possible, and it is the goal for every follower of Christ.

In the pages of this short letter, the apostle Paul writes to the Philippian church to "have this mind among yourselves, which is yours in Christ Jesus."

Paul is telling the believer that because of the indwelling of the Holy Spirit, we actually have the power to think Jesus-thoughts! *Are you kidding me?!*

There is no such thing as an insignificant thought. We are the product of hundreds, even thousands, of daily thoughts. However, if you dig under the thoughts of dry cleaning, spreadsheets, e-mails, or what you should eat for lunch, you will find some driving, consuming thoughts—thoughts that you attempt to keep tucked away, but the consuming thoughts remain. We serve a perfect God who is rightly jealous for His own glory. And if our thoughts shape our lives, no longer can we dismiss what we allow to bounce around in our minds. We have a very serious problem on our hands.

> Realizing this, we can no longer casually dwell on fears . . .
>
> We obsess over idols.
>
> We aren't merely "distracted" with worry . . .
>
> We are fixated on not trusting God.

Welcome to what I believe to be the greatest war we may ever fight: the war in our minds.

WE HAVE HELP

Here we sit in a post-truth society bombarded with promises of happiness, wealth, fulfillment, and all our dreams met. Yet so many of us are miserably unhappy. Why?

> ## Because for all the good that self-help does, that help always comes up short in the end.

The best that self-help can do with our suffering, with our shortcomings, with our spiraling is to reject it, to determine to do better, to declare, "Today this awfulness stops!"

But we don't simply need our spiraling thoughts to stop; we need our minds to be *redeemed.*

▶ Bondage necessitates rescue.

▶ Oppression needs to be lifted.

▶ Blindness waits for sight.

▶ Waywardness must be transformed.

C. S. Lewis wrote something I cannot quit thinking about because it dismisses the idea that God sent His Son to make us a better version of ourselves.

> Mere improvement is not redemption, though redemption always improves people even here and now and will, in the end, improve them to a degree we cannot yet imagine. God became man to turn creatures into sons: not simply to produce better men of

the old kind but to produce a new kind of man. It is not like teaching a horse to jump better and better but like turning a horse into a winged creature.[1]

This work we are going to do might be the most important thing we've ever done. But we don't do it merely as another self-improvement project. I want to become the winged creature, the "new kind of man." Don't you? The one who sets her mind on Christ, better yet realizes she has already been given the mind of Christ, and therefore, is deeply and intrinsically motivated and moved by an entirely different source. Not only do I make Jesus happy, but I find my complete happiness in Him. These are truths that if we could only believe, would change everything.

WHAT IS AT STAKE?

It is possible to waste our lives if we never learn to take our thoughts captive. Your thoughts produce actions that echo out into eternity. If you shut down because of the noise in your head, untold generations of kingdom builders could be missed. The enemy of our souls knows this—and nothing would give him greater happiness than seeing us stuck, wasting, spinning, instead of growing and walking forward in God's good purposes. This is how he operates. Your mind is the front line of this war. So don't let anyone tell you that your thoughts don't matter.

"So we learn to 'take captive every thought to make it obedient to Christ'" (2 Corinthians 10:5 ESV).

YOUR THOUGHTS MATTER!

But taking every thought captive feels very difficult . . . so let's start with taking one captive.

One little thought, that if you fully embrace it, will tip over like the first domino in a long line.

God gave you a choice. This one little thought could shift all the others. You get to interrupt the chaos and remember that you are "no longer a slave" (Galatians 4:7). You are free to live as a child and therefore an heir of God. And with that comes a lot of privilege and power. You get to decide moment by moment what you live for. And as heirs of God we get to live for Him!

You have a choice.

You are not a victim to your thoughts.

ENEMIES & WEAPONS	
In these weeks together, we will study the Scriptures and examine how we can use the following weapons to fight the enemies of our mind.	
ENEMIES	**WEAPONS**
Self-Importance	Humility
Noise	Silence
Cynicism	Delight
Isolation	Connection
Complacency	Intentionality
Victimhood	Gratefulness
Anxiety	Trust

SEE

▶ Watch video session 1 • INTRODUCTION • SPIRALING

▶ Use streaming instructions on inside cover or DVD.

▶ Take notes if you like.

ASK

▶ Use session 1: SPIRALING OUT Conversation Cards for group discussion.

▶ Complete the STUDY section for Introduction and Session 2 before your next group meeting.

STUDY

BACKGROUND ON THE BOOK OF PHILIPPIANS[2]

We're about to dive into the book of Philippians and see how Paul thought. Before we do, let's explore Paul's state of mind as he was writing to the church in Philippi.

ABOUT PAUL (THE AUTHOR)

▶ Paul was actually born as Saul. He was born in Tarsus in Cilicia around AD 1–5 in a province in the southeastern corner of modern-day Turkey.

▶ He was of Benjamite lineage and Hebrew ancestry (Philippians 3:5–6).

▶ His parents were Pharisees—fervent Jewish nationalists who adhered strictly to the Law of Moses—who sought to protect their children from "contamination" from the Gentiles.

- Saul went on to become a lawyer.

- Saul of Tarsus was a religious terrorist. Acts 8:3 states, "He began ravaging the church, entering house after house, and dragging off men and women, he would put them in prison."

- Of the 27 books in the New Testament, 13 are attributed to Paul.

- He was born about the same time as Jesus (c. 4 BCE) or a little later. He was converted to faith in Jesus Christ about 33 CE, and he died, probably in Rome, circa 62–64 CE.

- His trade was tent making, which he continued to practice after converting to Christianity.

THE CITY OF PHILIPPI[3]

- Philippi was a leading city of the district of Macedonia and was a Roman colony (Acts 16:12). Because of its location, Philippi became a center for trade.

- Greek was widely spoken.

- The citizens enjoyed treatment as if they were Roman citizens.

- Amphipolis was the capital of the district, and Thessalonica was the capital of the province.

PAUL WRITES THE LETTER

▶ Paul is in a Roman prison, likely with an execution sentence on his head.

▶ The context of the letter is the story of Epaphroditus, a Philippian believer, who was sent to Paul with a gift from the Philippians while Paul was in jail, and he sent this letter back to the church to say thank you and to encourage the young church.

THE CHURCH IN PHILIPPI

▶ The story of the start of the church in Philippi is found in Acts 16.

▶ Paul is very affectionate toward this church. He believes in them and wants to encourage them.

▶ Philippi was the first town in which Paul preached after he crossed the Aegean Sea from Troas and entered what we now call Europe. At that time, in AD 50, the city had few Jewish residents, and the first converts were Lydia, a Gentile businesswoman from Thyatira in the province of Asia Minor, and the Philippian jailer. The church evidently met in Lydia's home at first (Acts 16:15).

▶ Paul's companions on his first visit to Philippi included Silas, Timothy, and Luke.

▶ The Philippian Christians sent financial support to Paul in Thessalonica more than once (Philippians 4:15–16).

▶ Paul likely visited Philippi again, during his third missionary journey, in AD 57. He traveled from Ephesus to Corinth by land, and then from Corinth back to Miletus, mostly by land. From there he took a ship to Jerusalem. The land route he took on both occasions would have led him through Philippi.

PROJECT
CONSIDER

In this study we are going to talk a lot about the way we think and the way God has called us to think. But we rarely stop and even think about our thinking. We begin by being aware of what we are thinking about, by starting with what is true. Evil never wants to be noticed, I should mention here. It sneaks in and hijacks our minds, and we barely notice anything's amiss. So a vote for noticing. For thinking about what we're thinking about.

Here is your chance.

As we begin on this journey together I want you to take ten minutes to reflect on your thoughts and answer a few questions.

MIND MAP

STEP 1

Below, write down ten things you've spent the most time thinking about today.

1.

2.

3.

4.

5.

6.

7.

8.

9.

10.

▶ What are the primary emotions you tie to or associate with those things?

▶ Now take the most prevalent emotion and write it at the center of the blank space on page 28.

It could be good or bad.

You might write *anxious.* Or *peaceful. Overwhelmed. Angry. Afraid.*

Whatever it is, jot it down. Now draw a big circle around that word.

Scattered around that large circle, write everything you can think of that is contributing to that feeling or emotion. You might write "Laundry that isn't done" or "Work" or "Kids" or "Financial stress" or "Body image issues." Draw a smaller circle around each of these contributing factors; then trace a line from each of them, connecting them to the large one. Keep going until you have exhausted all the possibilities prompting the emotion you wrote down.

Here's an example of what one such mind map could look like:

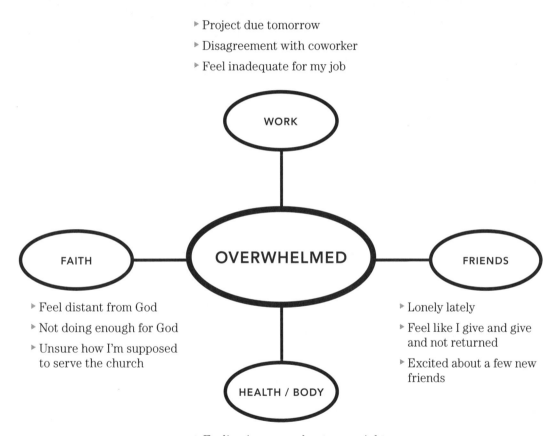

▸ Project due tomorrow
▸ Disagreement with coworker
▸ Feel inadequate for my job

WORK

OVERWHELMED

FAITH

FRIENDS

▸ Feel distant from God
▸ Not doing enough for God
▸ Unsure how I'm supposed
  to serve the church

▸ Lonely lately
▸ Feel like I give and give
  and not returned
▸ Excited about a few new
  friends

HEALTH / BODY

▸ Feeling insecure about my weight
▸ Worried about the doctor appointment
▸ Anxiety has been flaring up lately

▶ Draw your mind map here.

STEP 2

Talk to God about it. Pray with your map in front of you and talk through each thing you've written down. Tell Him about it. Ask Him to show you what you are believing wrongly about Him and yourself.

Ready to move on?

STEP 3

Look for patterns and common themes in your circles.

Are you worrying about things you cannot control?

Are you angry about how you've been wronged?

Are you obsessed with what you don't have?

Has food, sex, entertainment, or money taken over your thoughts?

Are you ashamed of what you've done in the past?

Are you self-critical?

▶ If you were to make one shift in the way you think, what would it be?

▶ This week keep a daily log of what you notice about where you mind spends its time. What themes emerge?

M _____

T _____

W _____

R _____

F _____

▶ What's the power in noticing? How can that start to change things?

▶ What is your relationship with Jesus like TODAY?
Describe honestly and consider how it is connected to
your thinking.

SCRIPTURE MEMORY

Over the course of this study we are going to memorize one of the greatest passages in the Bible. No other passage lays out the gospel quite so beautifully and concisely.

PHILIPPIANS 2:5–11 (ESV)

"Have this mind among yourselves, which is yours in Christ Jesus, who, though he was in the form of God, did not count equality with God a thing to be grasped, but emptied himself, by taking the form of a servant, being born in the likeness of men. And being found in human form, he humbled himself by becoming obedient to the point of death, even death on a cross. Therefore God has highly exalted him and bestowed on him the name that is above every name, so that at the name of Jesus every knee should bow, in heaven and on earth and under the earth, and every tongue confess that Jesus Christ is Lord, to the glory of God the Father."

Make a Scripture memory card with these verses on it and tape it on your mirror or anywhere else you'll see regularly. Read it, say it out loud, and repeat it every day.

SESSION 2

MAKE THE SHIFT

Work through pages 36–55 on your own before your next group meeting and before you watch the next video teaching.

Are you ready for a shift?

Ever wonder why it seems some people are happier than you, even if they are going through more difficult circumstances than you? Maybe you have visited Christians in developing countries thinking you were there to minister to them in their need, only to realize that in their smile and joy and selflessness, you were the one who had the need.

Yeah, me too.

When Paul wrote Philippians, the greatest exposition on joy ever written, he was actually bound in chains under house arrest. Paul apprehended something our cocoon-existence-of-comfort-in-the-West can never provide.

So this begs a second question.

What are you looking toward to make you happy?

Whether it is opioids or people's praise, whatever causes you to experience strong emotions of either happiness or disappointment—that is likely the thing you are living for. And it is very likely ruining your life.

I remember listening as a woman confessed extreme anxiety over her kids and their futures. She was brave to say it out loud, and I listened and I related and I prayed. She was looking at me asking, "What do I do?"

But actually I think the better question is, "Who is God?"

You see, if God is good, and loving, and in control, you can put your head on your pillow even with chaos swirling and the people you love out of your control, because you know Him and you know He has them, and He has you. He has all of it. Now, this is easier preached and harder lived, but that's why we are going to stick together and steep in God's Word these next five weeks. Change is difficult and may come slow—after all, these are ingrained thoughts and entangled sins. But because we have been made new creations, we have the Spirit's power and a choice to make. Changing our minds *is* possible. We do not have to spin.

If we're spiraling down toward our ultimate fixation, we can flip it. We can spiral up toward God instead.

This is what Paul did. If all Paul saw were his circumstances and his inability to change his imprisonment, he would surely have been despondent. But his circumstances didn't dictate his thoughts. It was his love of Jesus and trust in a good, loving, in-control God that consumed his mind and his purpose. And the same power that raised Christ from the dead, the same Spirit that empowered Paul to trust in the direst circumstances, is fully accessible for you and me. Right now. Are you ready for that shift?

ENEMIES & WEAPONS

In these weeks together, we will study the Scriptures and examine how we can use the following weapons to fight the enemies of our mind.

ENEMIES	WEAPONS
Self-Importance	Humility
Noise	Silence
Cynicism	Delight
Isolation	Connection
Complacency	Intentionality
Victimhood	Gratefulness
Anxiety	Trust

STUDY

READ PHILIPPIANS 1

One of the most important tools you can possibly possess is the ability to sit down with only your Bible and a pen and paper and discover truth for yourself. I love creating tools to aid in that, but ultimately I want you to be building this muscle as we journey together. So before we go any further, we're going to focus on the three keys to effective personal Bible study:

▶ Observation—Teaching Content

▶ Interpretation—Study

▶ Application—Projects

Throughout this journey through Philippians, I am going to give you the opportunity to practice each of these. I use them in each of my studies, because it's so important to build confidence in you to practice these skills in your own time of Bible study.

READ PHILIPPIANS 1

Read chapter 1 once all the way through without writing anything. Then read it again. On your second read, begin to jot down words and phrases that jump out to you. Get ready—this letter reads like a "best of" list of favorite and most quoted verses in the Bible.

As you read chapter 1, respond to the below:

▶ Write down some of the things you see that Paul is grateful for.

▶ In verses 9 and 10 what does Paul want for the Philippians and why?

▶ Read verses 15-17. What is the problem and how does Paul reconcile this?

▶ Rewrite verse 21 in your own words.

▶ Verse 27 talks about a "manner of life worthy of the gospel." Describe what Paul means by this. Look at verses 27-30.

▶ Now read back through all of your responses and write down some themes. I want you to write a summary statement of Philippians 1.

Example: The goal of the enemy is to have us love more than God. God's desire is we love Him most.

PHILIPPIANS 1 SUMMARY STATEMENT

_____

_____

_____

_____

_____

_____

_____

_____

_____

_____

_____

_____

"You shall love the Lord your God with all your heart and with all your soul and with all your mind and with all your strength" (Mark 12:30 ESV).

J. I. Packer, in *Knowing God*, says,

> What were we made for? To know God. What aim should we set ourselves in life? To know God. What is the "eternal life," that Jesus gives? Knowledge of God. [John 17:3] What is the best thing in life, bringing more joy, delight, and contentment than anything else? Knowledge of God. [Jeremiah 9:23] What, of all the states God ever sees man in, gives Him the most pleasure? The knowledge of Himself. [Hosea 6:6][4]

"To live is Christ and to die is gain" (Philippians 1:21 NIV).

A consuming mission for Paul. "To live is Christ . . ." *is Christ*. What interesting phrasing. It's not primarily an action. It is a state of being. It is to be with and to allow Christ to be in and through and with me as I live. It is less of a hustle and more of a state of being.

My son Cooper is adopted from Rwanda, and there are times when he will say to me, usually when we are punishing him for something, "I don't want to be in this family anymore." His actions and words are trying to change something unchangeable. He is an Allen. It is his reality no matter how he feels about it and no matter how he acts or doesn't act.

Getting out of our own heads begins with understanding our position in Christ. We are His, and we live that out as a matter of fact . . . either aware and surrendered to that truth or in rejection to what is true.

To live "is Christ."

▶ *Our position is as a member of Christ's body.* "Now you are the body of Christ and individually members of it" (1 Corinthians 12:27).

▶ *Our minds are the minds of Christ.* "'For who has understood the mind of the Lord so as to instruct him?' But we have the mind of Christ" (1 Corinthians 2:16).

▶ *Our lives making Christ's appeal.* "Therefore, we are ambassadors for Christ, God making his appeal through us" (2 Corinthians 5:20).

The more we understand our position with Christ, in Christ, through Christ, the less we try hard and the more we surrender.

Surrender.

It is the least active thing you can imagine doing.

Today I was all worked up about something I could not control at work. I was in knots about it and honestly it consumed my mind and time and even my mood all day.

Tonight I fell into bed and exhaled. I gave up. I told God what was true all along: "I lay here at Your mercy."

We can hustle at His mercy; we can worry at His mercy or we can rest because of His mercy.

Being wholly surrendered to one thing will shift everything about us.

Whatever you find your mind most fixed on—that is the thing you are living for.

SPIRALS

Our spirals can go one of two ways: up toward God or down toward the thing we're fixating on. In the coming weeks we'll start examining and dissecting our spirals and what to do about them, but for now we need to know that direction is everything. We want to go up, not down.

Here's how a typical downward spiral looks.

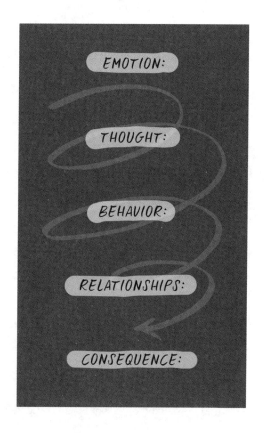

EMOTION:

THOUGHT:

BEHAVIOR:

RELATIONSHIPS:

CONSEQUENCE:

Our emotions trigger a thought. For example, feeling overwhelmed might make us think, *I'll never get through all this and there's no use trying*. Thoughts lead to behaviors (like numbing or procrastinating); behaviors affect relationships (like the ones we shut out or put off to nurse our overwhelmed minds); and then there are consequences. Friendships grow stale, opportunities are missed, we're left with things we don't want. But those things make up our lives. It can start to get out of control.

In this study we'll dig into each level on this spiral. But for now, know that when we spiral down, it's because we've *set our minds* on something that isn't God.

Here's what it looks like to spiral up instead:

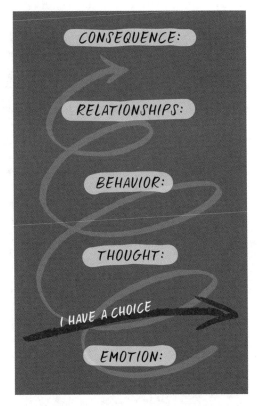

CONSEQUENCE:

RELATIONSHIPS:

BEHAVIOR:

THOUGHT:

I HAVE A CHOICE

EMOTION:

This spiral starts with a stance of surrender toward God that reminds us we are His, He is working through us, and we have a choice. So, when we're faced with the emotion that threatens to send us downward, we take hold of one thought: *I have a choice.* We learn to choose thoughts that conform to the mind of Christ; we start seeing better behaviors, better relationships, and better consequences. Our hearts are "set on what the Spirit desires" as Paul put it. Focused on God, our spirals begin to flip.

I love that Paul says we have a choice about what we think, no matter what the world is throwing at us. Often I sit down with women, and I hear their stories, and it doesn't matter what country or city we're in, the struggles are the same.

The people who stand out to me are the ones who have chosen to trust Jesus more than trusting their ability to make everything work out fine.

These heroes of the faith are not subject to their own thoughts.

They are not subject to their feelings.

They believe in one chief aim, and with every ounce of their power, they are working to think about Christ.

Jesus is the axis around which all their thought spirals spin. When their minds turn and turn, they fixate on Him. I want to learn to do the same.

WHO ARE YOU, LORD? & WHAT DO YOU WANT FOR ME?

Read Romans 8:5-11. In light of what you read, answer the questions above.

DIGGING DEEPER

(optional project for those of you wanting to go deeper)

WORD STUDY

▶ In Philippians 1:1 look up the Greek word for *servants*. Do a word study of that Greek word throughout the Bible.

▶ What does it mean that Paul used this specific word at the beginning of this book?

PROJECTS

I find it interesting that when Jesus was summarizing the desires of God for us He didn't leave it at "love the Lord God." He was clear that we are to love Him with all our heart and with all our soul and with all our mind and with all our strength. He was specific; and often in our study together of God's Word we let loving God with our minds be enough.

In the next few pages you will find a variety of projects. These projects are an effort to take what we learn in our minds into our hearts and souls and into our everyday lives. Some of these things may seem silly to you or uncomfortable. But these are the experiences that will hopefully reveal to us what our minds are consumed with and how we can conform our minds to Christ.

PROJECT 1
REFLECT

▶ Looking back at Romans 8:5–11, make two lists describing the mind set on the flesh and the mind set on the Spirit.

The mind set on the flesh	The mind set on the Spirit

PROJECT 2
CONSIDER

▶ Look back at your mind map from last session (pg. 24). Build five categories of thoughts you think about the most. And then narrow it down to one thing you've tried to live for. Let's give it a name.

My mind is most consumed with

How is that working for you?

1. _____

2. _____

3. _____

4. _____

5. _____

_____

(What is the one thing you're tempted to live for?)

PROJECT 3
RESPOND

▶ What circumstances has God put in your life that might be difficult, but could "advance the gospel" (Philippians 1:12)?

▶ Now, as Paul wrote to the Philippians giving them perspective on his situation, write someone you love a letter and give them perspective on how God is using this situation in your life. It doesn't matter if you ever send it. This exercise will help shift your perspective.

PROJECT 4
IMAGINE

▶ Look back at Project 2. Write the one thing that you are tempted to live for in the blank box. In the left column, write how your mind consumed with that thing is affecting each category below. In the right column, write how your mind consumed with Christ affects the same categories. Do you see the difference?

		CHRIST
Friendships		

		CHRIST
Family		
Work		
Time		
Joy		

CONCLUSION

What if we're missing the main thing—the best parts of life? Remember Christ is not after something from us, He is after something for us. He wants us to be free, free to enjoy Him, free to fully love people, free to live out the good works that He prepared in advanced for us to live. Very little is required from us, except *everything*. As we let go of everything and love God most, our minds and our lives shift and our spirals flip.

▶ What is the thought you are laying down this week?

▶ And what truth are you replacing it with?

SEE

▶ Watch video session 2: MAKE THE SHIFT

▶ Use streaming instructions on inside cover or DVD.

▶ Take notes if you like.

ASK

▶ Use session 2: MAKE THE SHIFT Conversation Cards for group discussion.

▶ Complete the STUDY section for Session 3 before your next group meeting.

WEAPONS WE USE

PART 1

Work through pages 60–83 on your own before your next group meeting and before you watch the next video teaching.

Remember, the greatest spiritual battle of our generation is being fought between our ears. This is the epicenter of the battle.

SO I'm going to train you to fight. I'm going to give you weapons.

To help you make the shift from negative, fleshly, worldly thinking to the clean, simple, straightforward thinking the apostle Paul talked about—thinking that reflects the mind of Christ.

That's what we're going to do over the next several weeks. We are going to look closely at our spirals and retrain our minds to interrupt our spirals. As we go to war with each toxic thought, we will begin to see the fruit and freedom of believing truth, walking moment by moment in our identity as children of God. The spiraling, chaotic thoughts that have so long kept us trapped will give way to the peace and beauty and abundant life Jesus died to give us.

Over the next two weeks, we'll dig deep into chapter two of Philippians, and discover that Paul gives us weapons to fight. These weapons might blow your mind, because we don't think of them as particularly "powerful" or "aggressive" concepts. But they are.

In Philippians 2, Paul is urging to the Philippian church to empty themselves for others, gloriously embodied by Christ's submission to God by taking on the form of man and laying down His life for God's glory and our good.

You see, Paul understands the human condition and he knows the struggle of the Philippian church. It's our struggle too. We don't want to think about others. Paul knows that our minds control our actions. Our bodies always move in the direction our head is turned.

The glory of God and the good of people. It is the opposite of the American dream and the opposite of everything our flesh craves. And Paul's words and Jesus' life in chapter 2 teach us it will be our only satisfying purpose and path to joy.

Made Himself nothing. Took on the nature of a servant. Humbled Himself. Obedient. Death on a cross.

If those phrases described a man, it would be a great act of self-denial, worthy of our attention. But how infinitely more powerful that those words describe God, the Son? Our response is only to bow down in worship and surrender our lives. If my Savior chose the cross over His comfort so I could be reconciled to God, then I CHOOSE others over myself. And it starts in my mind.

ENEMIES & WEAPONS

In these weeks together, we will study the Scriptures and examine how we can use the following weapons to fight the enemies of our mind. This week, let's look at humility, silence, and delight as choices we can make to stop our spiraling thoughts.

ENEMIES	WEAPONS
Self-Importance	**Humility**
Noise	**Silence**
Cynicism	**Delight**
Isolation	Connection
Complacency	Intentionality
Victimhood	Gratefulness
Anxiety	Trust

STUDY

READ PHILLIPIANS 2

▶ Describe the things that would make Paul's joy complete (verses 1-4).

▶ In verse 5 Paul is about to lay out the summary of the gospel. Who or what is Paul hoping this will impact?

▶ Summarize Philippians 2:6-11 in your own words.

▶ What are the results of worshiping and living like Jesus (verses 12-17)?

▶ In verses 19-30 note the ways in these verses that Paul says they lived differently than those who look out for their own interests:

▶ Look back at Romans 12:2:

"Do not be conformed to this world, but be transformed by the renewal of your mind" (ESV).

▶ How are we unlike the world? How do we become like Christ—living this opposite way?

We are transformed by the "renewal of our minds." We renew our minds by filling our minds with truth, with who God says we are, and then holding every other thought up to those truths. Those truths are our weapons, and they stop the spirals in our minds.

▶ THE WEAPON OF HUMILITY

In the first half of Philippians 2, we get a true picture of humility. That's our weapon against what Paul describes in the second half, all the mental, emotional, and relational chaos that comes from things like grumbling and complaining, anger and arguing, and an "every man for himself" kind of independence that only serves to promote greater angst.

One of the enemies of our minds specifically rampant in this generation is the inflated view of self being handed to us all over social media, in the shows and movies we watch, even in the self-help books we read. We're fed a continuous message of how much we matter, how very important we are—but in the long run, our urge to protect ourselves and promote our own awesomeness leads to more separation, more disillusionment with each other, and more insecurity and fruitless comparison.

We can make a different choice.

Lasting joy will come only when God is in the center. Not when I am empowered but when I rest in His power.

Here's how humility cuts through the spirals that can come out of us trying to be "better than":

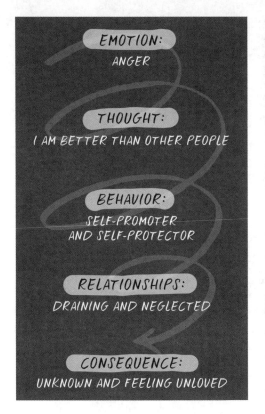

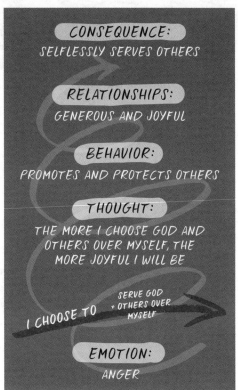

▶ Have you ever struggled with a spiral like this? How could choosing humility change things?

▶ THE WEAPON OF SILENCE

Humility is impossible unless we quiet the chatter and the noise and sit with Jesus. He's the source of our power. There can be no fighting until we're quiet with Him. Silence, in itself, is the most basic and intimate form of humility. We lay down everything and just stop—because we know He is greater.

Plus, in the stillness and quiet, not only do we connect with God but we are also able to more clearly identify what is wrong. Recognizing our spirals and naming them is the first step in interrupting them. That's why the enemy wants to fill our lives and our heads and hearts with noise. Because silence with God is the beginning of every victory.

Stillness, solitude in the presence of God, is the basis of our strategy for interrupting all kinds of problematic thought patterns.

Let's say that you're buried under a pile of stress and angst because of some situations at work. Here is how the thoughts probably churn their way through your mind:

I'm upset *because* I was passed over for the promotion I deserved.

I'm stressed *because* I'm working overtime yet not making ends meet.

I'm anxious *because* I'm running behind on my project and letting people down.

Now, you'll notice a pattern in each of these thoughts:

[Negative emotion] *because* [reason].

There are plenty of distractions awaiting to help you numb this frustration and stress. But here's where you get to use the weapon of silence. In silence, we get to rewrite that pattern while taking back the power He has given us. In other words, we can cognitively reframe our situations with the new pattern looking like this:

[Negative emotion], *and* [reason], *so I will* [choice].[5]

Here is how those thoughts can be changed.

I'm **upset**, *and* **I was passed over**, *so I will* choose to **remember** that God has not forgotten me.

I'm **angry**, *and* **she was rude**, *so I will* choose to **meditate** on God's kindness toward me.

I'm frustrated, *and* **I didn't keep my commitment to myself**, *so I will* choose to **look up verses** on God's mercy toward me and how it's new every single day.

When you're stuck in a downward spiral of discontent and distraction, get quiet. What truth will you shift your thoughts toward, in order to combat the lie that anything else can satisfy you like spending time with God?

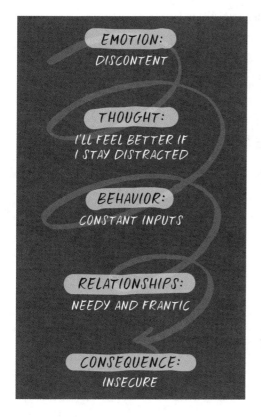

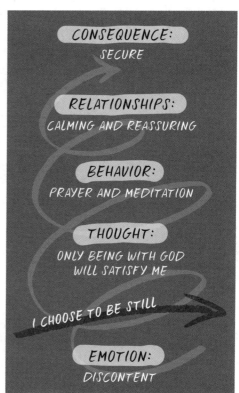

▶ THE WEAPON OF DELIGHT

In verse 17 of Philippians 2, after instructing his friends to do everything without grumbling and complaining, Paul invites them to be glad and rejoice. Though he's being "poured out like a drink offering" in jail, he offers a powerful choice. It makes me think. How often have we *chosen* to be unhappy? Rather than seeing the best and celebrating the good, we have chosen to see only the struggles and grumble and complain about the bad.

Who wants to live that way?

The enemy's strategy is to flood our thoughts with visions of all that is wrong in this broken, fallen world to the point we don't even think to look for the positive anymore. We get cynical. But God has an abundance of joy and delight for us, and we're missing it with arms crossed. What if there was another way to live?

When researchers studied awe and beauty, they found an interesting connection: when we experience awe, we move toward others in beneficial ways. We are freed from being the center of our own worlds for just a moment, and we become more invested in the well-being of others, more generous, less entitled.[6]

Stopping to delight in beauty is powerful. Cynicism says, "I'm surrounded by incompetence, frauds, and disappointment."

Delight is a weapon that tears down our walls and allows hope and worship to flood in.

And guess how worship springs up in us? When we look for delight instead of problems. We have that choice.

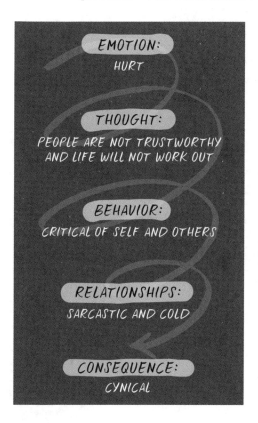

EMOTION:
HURT

THOUGHT:
PEOPLE ARE NOT TRUSTWORTHY
AND LIFE WILL NOT WORK OUT

BEHAVIOR:
CRITICAL OF SELF AND OTHERS

RELATIONSHIPS:
SARCASTIC AND COLD

CONSEQUENCE:
CYNICAL

CONSEQUENCE:
TRUSTING

RELATIONSHIPS:
ENGAGED AND CURIOUS

BEHAVIOR:
BELIEVES THE BEST IN OTHERS

THOUGHT:
GOD IS TRUSTWORTHY AND WILL, IN
THE END, WORK ALL THINGS OUT

I CHOOSE TO DELIGHT

EMOTION:
HURT

WHO ARE YOU, LORD? & WHAT DO YOU WANT FOR ME?

Read Psalm 19:1-6. In light of what you read, answer the questions above.

DIGGING DEEPER

(optional project for those of you wanting to go deeper)

WORD STUDY

For those of you who love to pull out your Greek dictionaries and
commentaries (or your Google searches), let's look at one of the theme words
in Philippians, *humility.*

> "Do nothing from selfish ambition or conceit, but in humility count
> others more significant than yourselves. Let each of you look not only
> to his own interests, but also to the interests of others. Have this mind
> among yourselves, which is yours in Christ Jesus" (Philippians 2:3–5
> ESV).

The following are some verses that build out the idea of humility in a deeper
way. Notice how Paul's passion for this is described in these passages:

▶ Ephesians 5:21

▶ Romans 12:10

▶ Ephesians 4:2

HUMILITY: A condition of lowliness or affliction in which one experiences a loss of power and prestige. Outside of biblical faith, humility in this sense would not usually be considered a virtue. Within the context of the Judeo-Christian tradition, however, humility is considered the proper attitude of human beings toward their Creator. Humility is a grateful and spontaneous awareness that life is a gift, and it is manifested as an ungrudging and unhypocritical acknowledgment of absolute dependence upon God.[7]

PROJECT 1
DELIGHT

Get outside, even if it is simply a blanket laid in your backyard and put in your

headphones and play some of your favorite worship music.

Reread Psalm 69 and Philippians 2 and dwell on all that Christ has done for you.

Simply be with Him. Thank Him. Delight in Him.

▶ What was this experience like for you?

PROJECT 2
CONSIDER

Draw a picture of you with everything you could ever want for yourself. This is an invitation to go a hundred percent "me me me" here. Put it all in the square. This should be fun! Stick figures and titling your little images are great!

▶ Now stare at that picture. What if you really got it all today? Would it make you happy?

The enemy has tricked us into believing that it would. But true joy is laying down all we could ever want, in humility.

"For I have told you often before, and I say it again with tears in my eyes, that there are many whose conduct shows they are really enemies of the cross of Christ. They are headed for destruction. Their god is their appetite, they brag about shameful things, and they think only about this life here on earth. But we are citizens of heaven, where the Lord Jesus Christ lives. And we are eagerly waiting for him to return as our Savior" (Philippians 3:18-20 NLT).

PROJECT 3
INVENTORY

We're going to take an inventory of the health of our thought patterns.

Color in where you feel you fall on the sprecturms below considering each category statement.

"1" being "I don't do this well."—"10" being "I'm great at this!"

HUMILITY VS. SELF-SERVING

Even when difficulties arise, I find myself grateful.

1	5	10

I quickly notice and communicate hurt or disappointment in my life.

1	5	10

I celebrate when people around me succeed.

1	5	10

I'm content when my work is not noticed.

1	5	10

I am relaxed when I cannot control my day.

1	5	10

Now, color in below where you fall.

"1" being "Not a problem"—"10" being "Ugh, That's Me."

DELIGHT VS. CYNICISM

I get annoyed when people are optimistic.

1	5	10

When someone is nice to me, I wonder what that person wants.

1	5	10

I constantly feel misunderstood.

1	5	10

When things are going well, I'm waiting for the bottom to fall out.

1	5	10

I quickly notice people's flaws.

1	5	10

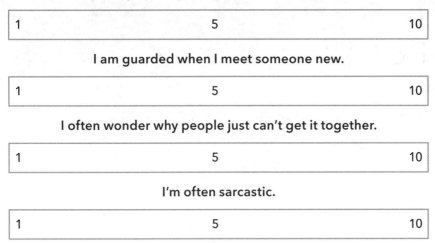

I worry about getting taken advantage of.

1	5	10

I am guarded when I meet someone new.

1	5	10

I often wonder why people just can't get it together.

1	5	10

I'm often sarcastic.

1	5	10

▶ Do any of these diagnostics correspond directly to the things that make you spiral? How might the weapons of humility and delight flip things around for you?

PROJECT 4
BE STILL

▶ Look back at your mind map on page 24 and consider your spiraling thoughts. In what ways can simply stopping, getting still, and thinking about God shift these spiraling thoughts?

CONCLUSION

Being single-minded is impossible unless we have something to focus on that is worthy of consuming our every thought and hope and dream. Only One thing in all of life cannot be exhausted by our complete focus and attention—the One who created us and died for us.

> "O God, you know my folly; the wrongs I have done are not hidden from you" (Psalm 69:5 ESV).

All of our thoughts are not yielded to God. In fact, if anyone knew half of what goes down in our heads, we'd have no friends. But this is the beauty of the gospel—it is both worthy of our full selves and able to reconcile ourselves back to Christ.

It is beautiful and transformative. The gospel forgives our folly and resets us in new ways every morning, because His mercies are new every morning. We get fresh starts again and again and again and again and again! We're gonna be all over the place all of our lives, but if we can have the posture and discipline of single-mindedness, the desire to please God, the desire to shift, He will transform us.

In my imagination I picture heaven full of service, because that is actually when I am most fulfilled, most connected to Jesus and to other people. We were built for this! Our joy comes from the very thing that we think might steal it . . . laying down our lives.

SEE

▶ Watch video session 3: WEAPONS WE USE, PART 1

▶ Use streaming instructions on inside cover or DVD.

▶ Take notes if you like.

ASK

▶ Use session 3: WEAPONS WE USE, PART 1 Conversation Cards for group discussion.

▶ Complete the STUDY section for Session 4 before your next group meeting.

SESSION 4

WEAPONS WE USE

PART 2

Work through pages 88-111 on your own before your next group
meeting and before you watch the next video teaching.

About a year ago, I noticed I was not very joyful. I was heavy all the time and there were a lot of reasons for it. I changed around a dozen things in my life, but one of the simplest changes I made was to remove all negative social media from my phone.

Our inputs matter. We are largely a product of our inputs. A few of my regular, subtle inputs were full of grumbling and arguments. It was turning me into a cynical complainer rather than a humble servant. I was concerned more about news stories than souls. I was distracted by loud, brash commentators on passing issues rather than sensitive to quiet, faithful world changers in the trenches of the real-life church.

The shift for me was small, but it transformed my mind to walk away from the things of this world and toward the quieter narrative God was unfolding around me. My inputs shifted and so did my thoughts. I found myself praying more because I was thinking more about Jesus and His people. Hope wasn't hard to drum up when I was constantly serving and with people who were sacrificially building the church. People like Pastor Andrew from Rwanda, who is in the States learning his Bible at seminary. He is away from his wife and children for years, all because he knows the pastors in his country need better theological training.

Last night Zac and I hopped in the car and ran Pastor Andrew a warmer coat and some chili because it is cold in Dallas, in mid-October! And being around him with his huge smile and heart, even though he is alone in a little dorm room in a cold, new city, my mind was renewed that God is at work across this planet.

Why did this feel so good? Because we weren't made to always be consuming—entertainment, arguments, distractions, material goods . . . pick your poison. But what if in those moments, we reached out to people—real live people in our lives—instead of diving deeper into the spirals in our own heads? We were, in fact, made for this. Made for connection. Made for service. Made for gratefulness. This world so in love with grumbling and complaining cannot hold a candle to the joy these things bring. So this week, we're going to explore these gifts God gave us. And we'll find out that they're actually weapons too.

I hope you're getting comfortable with Philippians 2 and are starting to realize how surprising things like humility, silence, and delight act as powerful weapons. We're going to park it here for another week, because it brings out three more ways to fight. And they're all about busting out of our comfort zones. Our enemy seeks to suck away our power with things like isolation, dissatisfaction, and complacency. We get nice and comfy, our worlds spinning around ourselves. When we wake up and reach out, we find that God has a much bigger work in mind than we could dream of—and we get to be part of it.

ENEMIES & WEAPONS

In these weeks together, we will study the Scriptures and examine how we can use the following weapons to fight the enemies of our mind. This week, let's look at connection, intentionality, and gratefulness as choices we can make to stop our spiraling thoughts.

ENEMIES	WEAPONS
Self-Importance	Humility
Noise	Silence
Cynicism	Delight
Isolation	**Connection**
Complacency	**Intentionality**
Victimhood	**Gratefulness**
Anxiety	Trust

STUDY

READ PHILIPPIANS 2

This week let's zoom into the latter part of Philippians 2.

READ VERSES 14–16.

▶ Describe the outcomes of eliminating grumbling and complaining from our lives.

▶ Describe Paul's view of the sacrificial nature of his life and why is that worth it to him in verses 16-18?

▶ What did he want the Philippians to do in his suffering for the gospel?

Paul describes 2 important friendships in the last part of chapter 2. He did not live isolated.

▶ Describe what Timothy's friendship meant to Paul in verses 19-24.

▶ Looking at verses 25-30 describe Paul's relationship with Epaphrodites. Why did he value him? What did he hope is life connected to the Philippians lives would accomplish?

SHINE LIKE LIGHTS

Paul says one of the clearest results of truly believing and embodying the gospel is this, which you'll remember from last week:

"Do everything without grumbling or arguing, so that you may become blameless and pure, 'children of God without fault in a warped and crooked generation.' Then you will shine among them like stars in the sky as you hold firmly to the word of life" (Philippians 2:14–16 NIV).

The generation living crooked and depraved . . . we have that part down. But the church being blameless and pure and doing everything without grumbling and arguing . . . . Daaannnggg . . . we have some work to do.

We've talked a little about how grumbling and anger and arguing are some of the many enemies to our lives being a true reflection of Christ. If we are not surrendered to the will of God and our worship is misplaced, then we will never live the mission God built for us.

I see this in myself and in others in a few forms.

DISCONTENTMENT:

Focused energy on dissatisfactions with our circumstances or possessions or life stage. Left unresolved this becomes a complaining spirit without joy or gratitude.

DISILLUSIONMENT:

Disappointment with the things of God and the people of God. Left unresolved it turns to bitterness and eventually a cynicism and distrust of people and God.

DISCOURAGEMENT:

Doubt, fear, and criticism can come against us to the point of shutting us down.

DISENGAGEMENT:

Our own insecurities or our disappointment in others cause us to pull back and isolate in order to protect ourselves.

▶ Do you see any of these in your spirit right now?

These can each turn into deadly spirals. As much as we'd like to, we can't curl up on our couches, read the pages of a book, pray, and simply *will* our minds to change. God is concerned not only with the posture of our hearts but also with the people on each of our arms. In terms of fulfilling our mission in this life, we can't do anything worthwhile alone.

We were built to be seen and loved.

▶ THE WEAPON OF CONNECTION

The apostle Paul beautifully described this way of living below:

"If there is any encouragement in Christ, any comfort from love, any participation in the Spirit, any affection and sympathy, complete my joy by being of the same mind, having the same love, being in full accord and of one mind" (Philippians 2:1–2 ESV).

It's a lot of togetherness, right?

God purposefully places us in community so they can help us in the battle for our thought lives. When our mind maps are chaotic, our thoughts are spiraling, and our emotions are running the show, so often our escape plan involves simply reaching out, just whispering that little word, "Help."

We find ourselves in a generation that has made an idol out of the very thing God is calling us away from: independence. But often when we back away from others, it's because we're listening to lies about our worth. We're convinced we're not worth knowing. We're convinced if we were known, we would be rejected. We want to be alone with our shame, not to bother other people with our bummer problems. But that's just a spiral that leads to ultimate loneliness.

Here's how connection busts that spiral:

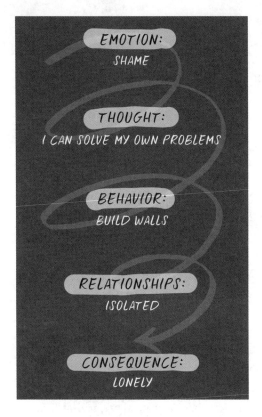

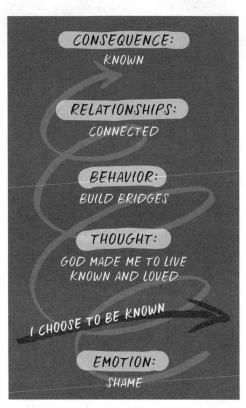

We weren't meant to be alone in the dark. Being known turns on the light. And that scares the devil. He doesn't want us in the light, because when we stay in the dark with him, he can tell us whatever he wants. No more. Use the weapon of connection, and fight with light.

▶ THE WEAPON OF INTENTIONALITY

We desperately want to be set free from the chaos of our minds—but set free to do what?

Our culture's idea about freedom is often that we are set free to do whatever we want. The irony is that when we go through seasons of doing whatever we want, those turn out to be our least content seasons. It all comes back to the same idea:

We were not built to live for ourselves.

I think of what Paul says about the Philippians—"everyone looks out for their own interests, not those of Jesus Christ"—and it reminds me of the eighteen months of doubt that held me captive. In that time, I just felt like doing whatever I wanted. Complacency overtook my naturally zealous spirit. Without a bent toward service, I bent toward too much Netflix, too much social media, too much sugar, too much grief. Click, scroll, binge, cry—rinse and then repeat.

I had no desire to go to the grocery store, let alone go to the nations with God's message of grace. You and I were made to be part of an eternal story centered on the unyielding purpose of our service to an unmatched God. We were meant to live intentionally rather than floating along, trying to be comfy.

Complacency is finding comfort in mediocrity, in accepting things as they are, clinging to the status quo. It's numbing and zoning out.

The questions driving our thought patterns are no longer *How will God use me today?* and *How can I give Jesus to someone?* Instead, we're focused on things like "What will make me feel better? What will make me look better? How can I feel okay and content?"

The apostle Paul gives us the weapon of truth that frees us from the velvet-covered chains of complacency:

"Do nothing out of selfish ambition or vain conceit. Rather, in humility value others above yourselves, not looking to your own interests but each of you to the interests of the others" (Philippians 2:3-4 NIV).

Intentionality is our weapon against complacency. We were meant to find joy in the work of God for others.

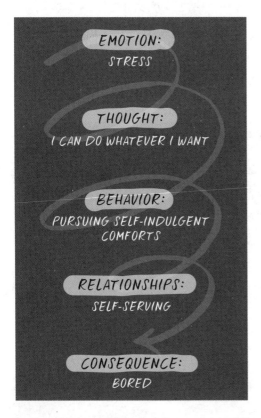

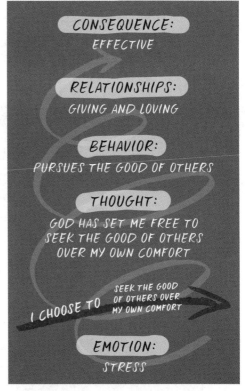

You know what our souls are saying to us? They're saying, "Comfy just ain't cutting it for me!"

There's a greater plan for service in our lives, and this is it. The way we fix our eyes on Jesus is to run the race set before us.

> We interrupt the spiral of self and the pattern of complacency when we serve intentionally.

▶ THE WEAPON OF GRATEFULNESS

The enemy offers us in a lineup of options that seem to comfort us but ultimately come up empty. One of those is the victim mentality.

I know. It's not comfortable to talk about. Especially since there is so much injustice in the world, and there are real victims who experience real suffering. We have to be about the business of righting these wrongs. Scripture implores us,

"Learn to do good; seek justice, correct oppression; bring justice to the fatherless, plead the widow's cause" (Isaiah 1:17 ESV).

I'm talking more here about spending so much time licking our wounds that we don't allow them to heal. We have to go from "victims" to "survivors." And that ultimately pulls us out of ourselves and connects us with each other.

We have a choice.

> We can center our thoughts on the certainty
> that, no matter what has happened to us,
> no matter what comes, we are upheld
> securely by God's righteous right hand.

And that will shift our minds toward gratitude.

We can choose gratefulness over victim mentality, because we are not victims of our circumstances; we are survivors, and held by God. Paul certainly made this choice, as evidenced by the fact that he was quick to express gratitude for the believers at Philippi despite the mind-boggling pain he'd endured. If anyone knew suffering, it was Paul.

In the book of Acts alone, we read that Paul experienced confrontation, the betrayal of friends, accusations, scourging, whippings, beatings, stoning, imprisonments, robberies, and on multiple occasions, being left for dead. Had any *one* of these things happened in the course of my lifetime, I'd center my whole world on the event. I'd tell *everyone* how bad it had been. In what has been dubbed our "victimhood culture," Paul certainly would have stood out.

I'm telling you, there's a far better way—the way of gratitude.

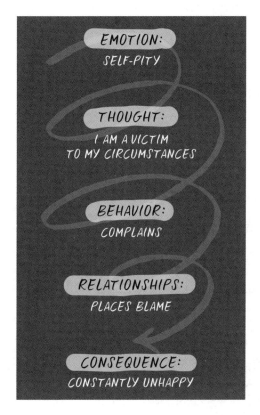
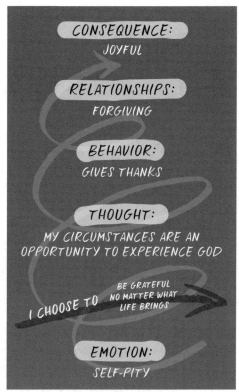

God made sure to include a clear call to thankfulness in Scripture.

God knows that only when we're
planted in the soil of gratitude will
we learn and grow and thrive.

WHO ARE YOU, LORD? & WHAT DO YOU WANT FOR ME?

Read Hebrews 3:12-14. In light of what you read, answer the questions above.

DIGGING DEEPER

In Acts 9:15–16 God told Ananias,

"Go, for he [Paul, also known as Saul] is a chosen instrument of mine to carry my name before the Gentiles and kings and the children of Israel. For I will show him how much he must suffer for the sake of my name" (Acts 9:15-16 ESV).

And suffer Paul certainly did.

In the book of Acts alone, we read that Paul experienced:

- ▶ having his life threatened in Damascus (9:23)

- ▶ having his life threatened in Jerusalem (9:29)

- ▶ being run out of Antioch (13:50)

- ▶ possible stoning at Iconium (14:5)

- ▶ stoning and being left for dead in Lystra (14:19)

- ▶ opposition and controversy (15:5)

- ▶ the loss of Barnabas, his friend and co-laborer in the gospel (15:39)

- being beaten with rods and imprisoned (16:22–23)

- being cast out of Philippi (16:39)

- having his life threatened in Thessalonica (17:5–7)

- being forced out of Berea (17:13–14)

- being mocked in Athens (17:18, 32)

- being apprehended by a mob in Jerusalem (21:27–30)

- being arrested and detained by the Romans (22:24)

- being imprisoned for more than two years in Caesarea (23:33–27:2)

- being shipwrecked on the island of Malta (27:48–28:1)

- a snakebite (28:3–5)

- being imprisoned in Rome (28:14–16)

- Pick a few of these instances and look them up to find out how Paul reacted and what he did in response. How would this be strikingly countercultural today?

PROJECT 1
INVENTORY

▶ What inputs in your life are stealing your joy? Inventory your inputs this week and how they actually make you feel.

▶ What happens in your mind when you dwell on Scripture and on what Christ has done for you?

▶ What happens in your mind when you move outward, toward other people?

"Women, 'Keep your heart with all vigilance, for from it flow the springs of life'" (Proverbs 4:23 ESV).

PROJECT 2
ASSESS

▶ Make a list of activities or experiences in the last week in which you have felt discouraged or cynical.

▶ Now look back at each moment and consider if or how your inputs have affected this?

▶ Describe how connecting with others could shift some of these patterns.

PROJECT 3
BUILD

We all need a team to help us when we feel like isolating. Someone on emergency speed dial to reach out to and say the word, "Help." Who in your life should be on this team?

Here are a few encouragements that may push you out of your comfort zone and help you find your people.

Seek Out Healthy People

▶ Are your people whole and healthy? I'm not saying perfect—but rather in touch with her strengths and weakness and clear on her values. Is she a good listener? Nobody's going to be 100 percent on this, but you're looking for emotional intelligence. And you have to *be* this kind of friend too. (Counseling's great if you're looking for ways to be healthier.)

Just Ask

▶ Just ask whether she'd like to connect! Coffee, a hike, board games with the fam, dinner before Bible study. Make it simple! It's easier than it sounds.

▶ Ask for help, advice, input. Ask until you don't cringe when asking people for something.

Say Yes

▶ Accept invitations. If you don't, they'll stop coming!

We can do life together only if we're actually *together* from time to time.

If you've become a decliner, try *yes* for a change!

Be All of You, Fast

▶ Bring the real you. Either I can "class it up" when I meet new people and pretend to be something I'm not. Or I can relish my wholehearted mess of a self with a good bit of self-deprecation and laughter and be at peace, just being myself with them.

In such brave endeavors, we may scare off the wrong people sooner, but we'll bring in the right people more quickly too.

WEAPONS WE USE, PART 2 • SESSION 4

Bother Others, and Let Others Bother You

▶ When you notice that your friend isn't herself, bug her until she shoots straight. Bother her until she feels safe enough to vent. She'll thank you for that bothering someday.

Likewise, to experience true community, you've got to be botherable yourself. Take the risk to trust someone with the truth of your life today.

Take initiative, and then let others take initiative with you.

PROJECT 4
SERVICE

This week plan a service project. Plan to serve somewhere, somehow alone or with your small group.

► Observe what happens in your brain and heart as you serve, and what happens in others. Write about it.

CONCLUSION

"Rejoice always, pray without ceasing, give thanks in all circumstances; for this is the will of God in Christ Jesus for you" (1 Thessalonians 5:16–18 ESV).

To see God's good purposes, we have to focus our gaze beyond our immediate situations. We have to remember that, even now, we have a choice: we can choose to praise and honor God right where we are, trusting that we serve a God who is both transcendent and immanent—fancy words for saying that His ways are beyond human understanding[8] yet He chooses to be near us, to be with us, even in the hardest times when we cannot yet see how He could possibly bring anything good from our circumstances. But as we build a grateful heart, we find purpose behind the pain. We see that God's purposes are only beginning, and we're freed from the spiral of victimhood. We don't have to define ourselves by others' wrongdoing. We choose to take back our power and our joy.

SEE

▶ Watch video session 4: WEAPONS WE USE, PART 2

▶ Use streaming instructions on inside cover or DVD.

▶ Take notes if you like.

ASK

▶ Use session 4: WEAPONS WE USE, PART 2
Conversation Cards for group discussion.

▶ Complete the STUDY section for Session 5 before
your next group meeting.

A NEW WAY TO LIVE

Work through pages 116–135 on your own before your next group meeting and before you watch the next video teaching.

My oldest went to college this year and, like all slightly crazed mothers, I tried to cram every last lesson into his precious mind in the final weeks before he moved out, as if this was the last legal time to preach to the poor kid.

Here was the last speech, the final words, my "sermon on the mount" (in the car) . . .

> "Son, you are light. I know this because I have seen God in you. I have seen you go from a selfish punk kid to a young man who responds to conviction. A young man who hears from God. You love people and you even put others ahead of your own interests. All of this is evidence that God is in you.

> "So you are light. It's a fact. It's your God-given identity as one of His kids. And you are headed into the pitch-black darkness.

> "There will be times you act like the darkness, but you will never *be* the darkness, and you will never be at home in the darkness again."

And team, same goes for us, if you know Jesus Christ as Savior. We have been given new life, new identities, and a new motivation. The light of Jesus resides in us and through us. No matter what spirals we face on a day-to-day basis. Yet, our flesh, the world, and the adversary are doing everything in their power to stymie us with our past.

We moved from being slaves to sin to being children of God. We will probably be trying to wrap our minds around this astonishing truth until we get to heaven.

But we must try because it shifts everything about us. As God's children, filled with the Holy Spirit, we *have* the mind of Christ, Paul tells us in 1 Corinthians 2:16; the issue is whether we're *using* it to think the thoughts that Jesus might think.

Are we taking every thought captive and training our minds daily in the right paths? Are we moving forward instead of looking backward?

Now that you know how to fight, we're going to talk about how to go the distance. How to persevere and keep growing in strength and maturity. In chapter 3 of Philippians, Paul is telling us how to mature in our thoughts. Paul is exhorting this young church to follow his lead; to follow his example of maturity as he fixes his mind on Christ. Why do we need to mature? Because we want Christ. Maturity as a Christian is the process of becoming more like Christ. And none of us are there yet.

And perhaps surprisingly, one of Paul's indicators of maturity is the discipline of *forgetting* what's behind so we can move on to what's ahead. So we can grab on to what's ours in Christ. Later in this lesson, we will process the why and how of forgetting.

But for now, let's go—Philippians 3.

STUDY

READ PHILIPPIANS 3

▶ Paul begins chapter 3 with a warning. What exactly is he asking the church to watch out for? (verses 2–4)

▶ List the things Paul says he could put his confidence in. (verses 4-6)

▶ What does Paul do with all of his most precious earthly gains? (verses 7-9)

▶ Why would he do this? (verses 10-11)

▶ Paul is going to challenge the mature followers of Christ (verse 15) to think a certain way in this passage. Read verses 12–16 and list the train of thought and action that Paul models here.

▶ Verse 17 says why we should think and act like Paul. What is the reason for Paul's hope?

▶ Read verses 18–19 and describe the enemies of the cross of Christ.

▶ In verses 20–21 Paul builds out our ultimate motivation for godliness. Describe it here in your own words.

▶ Summarize Philippians chapter 3 in your own words.

> "Those of us who are mature think this way" (Philippians 3:15 ESV).

In my research on biblical maturity it became clear, very quickly, that maturity was a subject Paul cared a lot about. No one in the Bible talks more about maturity than Paul. I know why. Because he was writing letters to a fragile young church, and his deepest desire was that this small flame of faith would catch ablaze and spread to the ends of earth. These first-generation believers had grown up in a culture and belief system different from the identity they now possessed, and Paul's letter to the Philippian church is discipleship from a distance.

Let's look at some of his key phrases connected to mature thinking. He draws from the imagery of a running race—having a vision of focused endurance to the finish line. No longer is Paul's finish line achievement or status.

Press on.

The phrase I want to come back to is **forgetting what lies behind**.

Straining toward what lies ahead.

Toward the goal, the prize, which is the call of God in Christ Jesus.

The phrase I want to come back to is "forgetting what lies behind." As we look to reign in our thoughts and mind, this is no small command. We are terrible forgetters when it comes to our past, aren't we? No matter if it was an achievement or a shameful decision, we too often allow our past to dictate our thoughts and lives. But Paul was addressing something deeper than his past actions and accolades; he was talking about his motivations. Forgetting what lies behind sounds impossible, doesn't it? Our brains never stop working, even when we sleep. So yes, it is impossible to only forget and be left with nothing in our minds.

How do we become great at forgetting?

WE BECOME EXPERTS IN REMEMBERING

Paul's single-minded goal was what motivated him to forget, to leave behind his past. Paul's new motivation was so consuming that he gave no value to his past—thus leaving no room for his past to define him. As long as we leave room in our minds for the past, we will allow it to define us.

When I sit down with a woman who genuinely loves Jesus and says she is not in bondage, yet I hear bitterness and unforgiveness . . . we have a problem. Because even though this is invisible bondage, it is bondage and a hindrance to focused endurance to the finish line. *And roots of bitterness and unforgiveness will not just fade away.* Every thought bears fruit.

So whatever does not produce the fruit of righteousness must be held up to the light of the gospel, to allow God to deal and heal.

And guess what happens when you get free from the past? You get free to run your race. Now for many of you, before you can move forward you need to process & forgive & work through difficult circumstances. Do the work, but then it is time to no longer be defined by it.

FORGETTING

"Keep your heart with all diligence, for from it flow springs of life" (Proverbs 4:23). The heart here can be defined as "the seat of our thoughts, will, and emotions." Who we are, our very intangible essence that makes us uniquely us, lives somewhere in the recesses of our mind.

So we, as maturing Christ followers, guard our minds because flowing out of it . . . comes every aspect of life.

What we think will directly become who we are.

So why do you have to become great at forgetting? Because you are a new creation, with a new identity, and a new motivation. And Jesus is just that good.

Some of you need to forget because your past is filled with how awesome you are, and you have built your identity on your ability and the applause of man, and you wonder why you don't feel like you need God or why you don't want to grow in maturity.

Some of you need to forget because you built your identity on your lack of awesomeness, and all you can do is think of yourself as well, but not in a good light. You can never imagine being confident enough to pour your life into another person.

Some of you have a past full of shame. Whether you were a victim or actively ran from God, your past still defines you and holds you in bondage, and your greatest fear is still being found out.

Forget what is behind . . . race toward what is ahead.

I know for some of you this sounds too simplistic. Seasons of difficulty in my life have required a lot of counseling till the gaping wounds have begun to heal. But the point is, we have to fight down the distractions and bondage that keep us from wholly advancing the gospel with every part of our lives. Let's become free people—because free people free people.

▶ So what do you need to forget or work through?

▶ What work needs to happen in your life to move toward that freedom?

▶ What is the first step in that work that you can do before this day is over?

WHO ARE YOU, LORD? & WHAT DO YOU WANT FOR ME?

Read Romans 7:15–25. In light of what you read, answer the questions above.

DIGGING DEEPER

(optional project for those of you wanting to go deeper)

WORD STUDY

Ready for a fun one?

▶ In Philippians 3:3 Paul talks about the believers in Philippi being the *circumcision*. Look up the Greek word for *circumcision* and study what that meant in Israel's history. What is Paul saying in verse 3 and how does it compare to what the believers of this day understood about religion and faith?

PROJECT 1
REFLECT

▶ Ask two people who know you best, "In what areas of my life do you see me needing to mature?" This is scary but will be very insightful.

PROJECT 2
CONSIDER

▶ *"Follow me as I follow Christ"*: Text somebody right now who has influenced your faith and tell them what they mean to you. How have they modeled being a mature follower of Christ to you?

PROJECT 3
CHANGE

Circle the thought pattern(s) and ways of thinking that entangle you.
All or nothing thinking
Sometimes called "black and white thinking." "If I'm not perfect I have failed." "Either I do it right or not at all."
Mental filter
Only paying attention to certain types of evidence. Noticing our failures but not seeing our successes.
Jumping to conclusions
There are two key types of jumping to conclusions: (1) Mind Reading—Imagining we know what others are thinking, and (2) Fortune telling—Predicting the future
Emotional reasoning
Assuming that because we feel a certain way, what we think must be true. "I feel embarrassed so I must be an idiot."

https://positivepsychology.com/cognitive-distortions/

Labelling

Assigning labels to ourselves or other people. "I'm a loser." "I'm completely useless." "They're such idiots."

Overgeneralizing

Seeing a pattern based upon a single event, or being overly broad in the conclusions we draw.

Disqualifying the positive

Discounting the good things that have happened or that you have done for some reason or another. "That doesn't count."

Magnification (catastrophising) and minimization

Blowing things out of proportion (catastrophizing), or inappropriately shrinking something to make it seem less important.

Should/Must

Using critical words like "should," "must," or "ought" can make us feel guilty, or like we have already failed. If we apply "shoulds" to other people the result is often frustration.

Personalization "This is my fault."

Blaming yourself or taking responsibility for something that wasn't completely your fault. Conversely, blaming other people for something that was your fault.

▶ Give some examples of how these thought patterns entangle you.

▶ What would it take to wrestle them to the ground?

PROJECT 4
EXPERIENCE

Visit a nursing home/older person and learn from them. Ask them the following questions and listen intently.

▶ What do you care about?

▶ What do you regret?

▶ What do you fear?

▶ What do you hope?

CONCLUSION

With each positive choice made—choosing stillness instead of distraction, for example, or community instead of isolation—we are training ourselves to use the mind of Christ that we have. The more we make these positive choices, the more reflexive that approach becomes. We said that at first such a shift is *possible* through consciously, deliberately interrupting our spirals. But as we practice more, that shift becomes *probable* and then *predictable* and then utterly *instinctive* to us. Eventually we get to the place where we don't even realize we're interrupting our negative thinking in order to choose mind-of-Christ thinking, because the impulse has become so ingrained.

I liken it to cutting a road in the woods. At first the path is marked by flattened leaves on foot-worn soil. But over time the demand for that path will cause someone to come in and pave and install mile markers. Eventually the path is so clear cut that it would be senseless to take another route. That path is just the path you always take.

It's not easy to stop believing lies. We can't simply sit back and wait for our minds to heal, for our thoughts to change. We train. We walk the path over and over again, pressing on toward what is ahead and forgetting what is behind. That's how truth gains the victory in the battle for our minds.

We stick our heads in our Bibles day in and day out. We are consumed with Jesus, and we keep moving. You might not be able to fully grab hold of truth at the beginning, but as you persevere, it will cut a path and become permanent.

We keep getting up and going to Jesus. Choosing to connect with him and make Him first. We keep interrupting our spirals with community, service, gratitude, every good choice.

We choose well. Daily. Moment by moment. We train our minds. And when a new temptation to spiral presents itself, we trust our training.

SEE

▶ Watch video session 5: A NEW WAY TO LIVE

▶ Use streaming instructions on inside cover or DVD.

▶ Take notes if you like.

ASK

▶ Use session 5: A NEW WAY TO LIVE Conversation Cards for group discussion.

▶ Complete the STUDY section for Session 6 before your next group meeting.

A MIND LIKE CHRIST

Work through pages 140-162 on your own before your next group meeting and before you watch the next video teaching.

Well, we've made it to the end, my friends. It's the last week of our time together, and we'll be in the last chapter of Philippians. This chapter is full of some of the most beloved verses in the Bible—a parting gift from a man who knew what it was like to have the mind of Christ. When he was giving encouragement to the Philippians, it's almost like Paul knew what we'd be wondering, at the end of such a life-changing and mind-changing journey: *What next? What about tomorrow? How do I keep doing this thing, day after day?*

So we have here some final, powerful weapons to help us into the future. To arm us against anxieties about our tomorrows, to encourage us in truth and in contentment, and get us ready for whatever may come. Because whatever it is, we're not going to do it in our own strength.

"I can do all things through him who strengthens me" (Philippians 4:13 ESV).

The secret is Christ's strength in us.

This verse was a chant we used to cheer at the summer camp I attended in my childhood. But honestly, I had absolutely no idea what it meant or how it was supposed to actually work. But we cheered it loudly and constantly. And it comforted me.

It comforts me still. But we need to dig deep into it now, as we go forward in the pursuit of a mind conformed and captivated by Christ, because we need help. A lot of help . . . Jesus knew this and made this promise:

"I tell you the truth: it is to your advantage that I go away, for if I do not go away, the Helper will not come to you. But if I go, I will send him to you. And when he comes, he will convict the world concerning sin . . . When the Spirit of truth comes, he will guide you into all the truth, for he will not speak on his own authority, but whatever he hears he will speak, and he will declare to you the things that are to come. He will glorify me, for he will take what is mine and declare it to you. All that the Father has is mine; therefore I said that he will take what is mine and declare it to you" (portions of John 16:7–15 ESV).

God knew we needed help and so He gave us that help in the form of the Spirit, who is living and active and changing those of us who have trusted in Christ.

"For who knows a person's thoughts except the spirit of that person, which is in him? So also no one comprehends the thoughts of God except the Spirit of God" (1 Corinthians 2:11 ESV).

And because we have access to His Spirit, the mind of Christ is ours! It's already in His Spirit living within us and laid out through His Word. We have help for our anxieties and fears about tomorrow. And permission to live the opposite of afraid: content.

Paul has a secret for contentment noted in the following scripture:

"I know what it is to be in need, and I know what it is to have plenty. I have learned the secret of being content in any and every situation, whether well fed or hungry, whether living in plenty or in want" (Philippians 4:12 NIV).

And the power of that in Paul was he lived *unafraid* of what the world could do to him. His confidence wasn't in his achievement or his possessions or how well his life was going . . . it was in His God.

I pray this for you. I pray that whatever God has ahead for you, that above all you would find the secret of contentment and joy that is to know and love and walk with Jesus.

It is the only single thing that satisfies and cannot be taken from you.

ENEMIES & WEAPONS

In these weeks together, we will study the Scriptures and examine how we can use the following weapons to fight the enemies of our mind. This week, let's look at trust as the choice we can make to stop our spiraling thoughts.

ENEMIES	WEAPONS
Self-Importance	Humility
Noise	Silence
Cynicism	Delight
Isolation	Connection
Complacency	Intentionality
Victimhood	Gratefulness
Anxiety	**Trust**

STUDY
READ PHILIPPIANS 4

▶ Describe Paul's view of the women he served with in verses 2-3.

▶ In verses 4-7 Paul talks about anxious thoughts and what to do with them. List his instructions and the result if these instructions are heeded.

▶ List the things Paul encourages us to think on. (verse 8)

▶ In verses 11–13 Paul writes about contentment. What is his secret?

▶ In what ways have you been brought low?

▶ In what ways have you abounded?

▶ What would contentment look like for you in each of these circumstances?

▶ What fears do you face going forward?

THE LAST SPIRAL

How many of us are dragging through our days, weighed down by anxiety? Many of us find our thoughts circling around problematic circumstances or people. For others of us, anxiety has become the soundtrack of our days, so familiar we hardly notice it playing in the background of every scene.[9]

As we look to our future, the enemy has ensnared us with two little words: "What if?"

With those two little words, he sets our imaginations whirling, spinning tales of the doom that lurks ahead.

But our tool for defeating "what if" is, not surprisingly, found in two words: "Because God."

Because God clothes the lilies of the field and feeds the birds of the air, we don't need to be anxious about tomorrow.

Because God has poured His love into our hearts, our hope will not be put to shame.

Because God chose us to be saved by His strength, we can stand firm in our faith no matter what the day holds.

Freedom begins when we notice what it is that is binding us. Then we can interrupt it with the truth.

Anxiety says, "What if?"

▶ *What if I get too close to this person and she manipulates me like the last friend I trusted?*

▶ *What if my spouse cheats on me?*

▶ *What if my children die tragically?*

▶ *What if my boss decides I'm expendable?*

▶ *What if . . . ?*

Certainly there are healthy levels of anxiety that signal our brains to be afraid of things that are truly worth being afraid of—like a wild animal or a train coming toward us on the tracks.

But "[i]t is when this life-saving mechanism is triggered at inappropriate times or gets stuck in the 'on' position that it becomes a problem."[10] Our fear goes into overdrive.

We keep finding new concerns to worry about and new facets to each concern, as if by constant stewing we can prepare ourselves for what's to come. But there is a God who will give us what we need today, next week, and twenty years from now, even if our very worst nightmares come true.

So we have a choice going forward. The enemy wants to tell us that we cannot trust God to take care of our tomorrows. But the truth is, God is in control of each and every day. And we do everything in His strength.

Here's the choice we make:

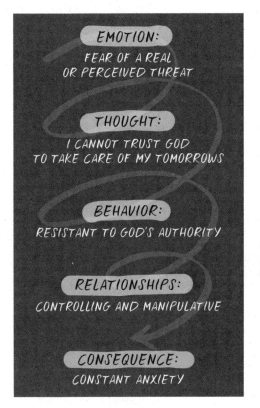

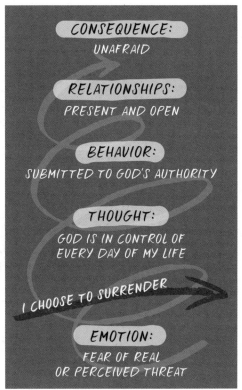

Paul knew we would spiral, so he told us to replace the lies with something surprising.

"Do not be anxious about *anything*, but in every situation, by prayer and petition, with thanksgiving, present your requests to God. And the peace of God, which transcends all understanding, will guard your hearts and your minds in Christ Jesus.

"Finally, brothers and sisters, whatever is true, whatever is noble, whatever is right, whatever is pure, whatever is lovely, whatever is admirable—if anything is excellent or praiseworthy—think about such things" (Philippians 4:6-8 NIV, emphasis added).

Anything?

Anything.

▶ How could Paul say that? Isn't that impossible? Does God really command this of us?

Paul meant what he wrote. He meant it for one simple reason: this earth is not our home, and our home in heaven is secure. So if death is not to be feared, what exactly do we have to be scared of?

God's promises give us ultimate hope in absolutely every circumstance. He meets every need. He will resolve (in the end) every problem we may face here on earth. Paul wrote in confidence of this truth, and then he gave us clear guidance for ridding ourselves of anxious thoughts:

1. Choose to be grateful.

2. Choose to think about what is lovely and excellent and true.

▶ THE WEAPON OF TRUST

We fight our anxious thoughts by trusting the God who knows all things and will give us what we need, exactly when we need it.

For just a moment, let's zero in on one of these replacement thoughts: "Whatever is true . . . think about such things."

If we want to focus on what's true, we've got to kick out the lies.

> God has called us to hope, to joy, to perseverance—to think on what is true!

Truth is the most powerful weapon we have against the enemy, who is "a liar and the father of lies." So we fight the enemy with whatever is true—meaning, whatever is real!

Women, we are not children of the devil. We are children of God, who reject the lies that have been swimming in our minds and replace them with the truth.

So what lies have you been believing? Chances are, they fall into one of these three categories:

1. *I'm helpless.*

2. *I'm worthless.*

3. *I'm unlovable.*

▶ Where did this lie come from? What's the earliest moment you remember believing it?

▶ How do these lies tend to play into your fears and anxieties?

We have to let God's love and His truth soak into our souls, over and over again. We seek Him, we pray, we sit with Him in silence, we walk with Him in our spiritual disciplines. And ultimately, we make a choice. We choose to believe the truth instead of a lie. Until I throw off the lie that God's love isn't for me, my emotions, decisions, behaviors, and relationships will remain twisted up in the mistaken belief that I'm worthless. So I focus on what is true.

FIGHT IT

Take one of the anxious thoughts you have running around in that head of yours and explore it on the grid below.

GRAB THE THOUGHT	DIAGNOSE THE THOUGHT
What is it?	**Is it true?**

TAKE IT TO GOD	MAKE A CHOICE
What does God say about it?	**Am I Going to believe God?**

I think most of us are probably good at finding the thought, recognizing it as a lie, and even knowing what the truth is. But we fail on the last step. We keep believing the lie, acting on it, letting the "what ifs" stir our thoughts into a frenzy.

But we have to go to war. We have to read God's Word and find every weapon available to fight it.

Yes, faith is a gift, but it is a hard-won gift at times. Paul wrote honestly of how God met him in his struggle: "He said to me,

> " 'My grace is sufficient for you, for my power is made perfect in weakness.' Therefore I will boast all the more gladly about my weaknesses, so that Christ's power may rest on me" (2 Corinthians 12:9 NIV).

With this kind of surrender, the ultimate result is surprising. It's contentment.

> **Contentment** is an inner sense of rest or peace that comes from being right with God and knowing that He is in control of all that happens to us (Steven Cole, Bible.org).

If you have ever spent time around Christians in developing countries, you have probably been mesmerized by their joy and contentment. We think living in the land of options and choices is how we can find happiness, but I think choices fill our mind space, robbing us of the opportunity to be content.

Contentment. It is our ultimate aim in life. As humans we search the earth for it. But Paul knows the secret, the place it hides, and he shares it with us.

WHO ARE YOU, LORD? & WHAT DO YOU WANT FOR ME?

Read 1 Corinthians 2:11-16. In light of what you read, answer the questions above.

DIGGING DEEPER

(optional project for those of you wanting to go deeper)

WORD STUDY

Look up the Greek words found in Philippians 4:8. How do these definitions expand your view of what we are to think about? As you study, consider how these words describe Christ.

{alēthē / truth, true}	Definition:
{semna / honorable}	Definition:
{dikaia / justice, righteous}	Definition:
{hagna / pure}	Definition:
{prosphilē / lovely}	Definition:
{euphēma / praiseworthy}	Definition:
{aretē / excellence}	Definition:
{epainos / worthy of praise}	Definition:

PROJECT 1
CONSIDER

Here is a grid to work through with some of your most nagging and common thoughts. Consider Philippians 4:8.

Whatever is true.	Is this thought true? Is what I'm worried about factual or imagined? Is what this person said of me/my identity true according to God's Word?
Whatever is honorable.	Is this thought meaningful and does it matter? Am I anxious over triviality? Are my thoughts beautiful and valuable?

Whatever is right.	Am I meditating on God's personhood and considering Him as my standard of morality? Are my thoughts a result of this pursuit or am I trying to model my behavior by culture and as a result, anxious, weary, and confused? Is this standard I've created for myself a holy standard or did culture set it for me?
Whatever is pure.	Are my thoughts, creativity, and imagination free from sin? Am I imagining evil scenarios and sequences? Am I filling my mind with movies, shows, books, music that are sexual or impure? What are my eyes taking in?
Whatever is lovely or worthy of praise.	Am I consuming and pursuing things of beauty? Am I seeking out art and majesty beyond myself? Am I finding ways to take in God's creation around me? Are my thoughts worthy of being written down and shared across the table with people around me? Am I contributing to making this world beautiful?

Whatever is admirable or excellent.	Am I believing the best in others despite the judgements I've created based on their words, appearance, or behavior? Are my thoughts toward someone based on facts or created/imagined scenarios? Am I choosing to feel excluded because I've created a storyline that someone thinks about me that is not actually true?

▶ How do these questions shift your perspective on your thought life?

PROJECT 2
RISK

Grab an hour with a trusted friend or family member and share with them the answers to these thoughts:

▶   I find myself thinking too much about . . .

▶   This bothers me because . . .

▶   My hope is to shift my thoughts to . . . Here is how you could help take my thoughts captive . . . It matters to me because . . .

PROJECT 3
DRAW

In the first box draw what you are leaving behind and in the second box draw what you are moving toward.

LEAVING BEHIND

MOVING TOWARD

PROJECT 4
DREAM

▶ Write a letter to yourself below. Tell yourself your hopes for your mind in the coming year. What do you want to shift? What is it going to take to get there?

CONCLUSION

"No natural feelings are high or low, holy or unholy, in themselves. They are all holy when God's hand is on the rein. They all go bad when they set up on their own and make themselves into false gods."

— C.S. Lewis, The Great Divorce

It's interesting, the reason Paul could write these words on contentment was he had experienced plenty, but he also had experienced what it means to be brought low.

It's always excruciating to watch my children be brought low, and it's excruciating when we are brought low. It's not what we hope for them or us. But tasting the low, the empty, the need, is what confirms what we pray is true.

It's true that Christ's strength really is enough for me.

That we can live with renewed minds, because of that strength. That we are not alone in the dark, but with friends in the light. He has made all these weapons available to us and has empowered us with His strength. So let's fight for each other! And with the power of healthy minds trained on Christ, we'll be contagious and bring light to others.

It is true that we can live with renewed minds. It's all true. And when we set our minds on truth, freedom follows.

SEE

▶ Watch video session 6: A MIND LIKE CHRIST

▶ Use streaming instructions on inside cover or DVD.

▶ Take notes if you like.

ASK

▶ Use session 6: A MIND LIKE CHRIST Conversation Cards for group discussion.

HOW TO FIND GOD

I can't imagine a more restless feeling than being unsure about the meaning of life and the future of my soul. As long as we are on this earth, we will ache for something bigger, because we were designed for something bigger—something better. We are designed for an intimate relationship with God forever.

Saint Augustine said, "You have made us for yourself, and our hearts are restless until they find their rest in you."[1]

We had a perfect relationship with God until sin entered the world through Adam and Eve. And with sin came the promise of death and eternal separation from God. But from the moment of the first sin, God issued a promise that would bring us back to him.

The penalty had to be paid.

Our sin was to be placed on a perfect sacrifice. God would send his own blameless, perfect Son to bear our sin and suffer our fate—to get us back.

Jesus came fulfilling thousands of years of prophecy, lived a perfect life, and died a gruesome death, reconciling our payment for our sin. Then after three days, he defeated death and rose from the grave and now is seated with the Father, waiting for us.

Anyone who accepts the blood of Jesus for the forgiveness of their sin is adopted as a child of God, and issued God's very own Spirit to seal and empower us to live this life for him.

---

1. Augustine of Hippo, *Saint Augustine's Confessions*, trans. Albert C. Outler (Mineola, N.Y.: Courier Dover Publications, 2002), 103.

Our souls are restless until they rest in God. We were made for him, and he gave everything so that our souls could finally and forever rest in him.

If you have never trusted Christ for the forgiveness of your sins, you can do that this moment. Just tell him your need for him and tell him of your trust in him as your Lord and Savior.

ENDNOTES

1. C. S. Lewis, *Mere Christianity* (San Francisco: HarperOne, 2015), 183–184.

2. GotQuestions.org. What Can We Learn from the Life of Paul? 31 Aug. 2018, www
   .gotquestions.org/life-Paul, html.

3. Philippians, www.planobiblechapel.org/tcon/notes/html/nt/philippians
   /philippians, htm.

4. J. I Packer, *Knowing God* (Downers Grove, IL: Intervarsity Press, 1993).

5. For more information on cognitive reframing, see Elizabeth Scott, "4 Steps to
   Shift Perspective and Change Everything," *VeryWell Mind*, June 16, 2019, (www
   .verywellmind.com/cognitive-reframing-for-stress-management-3144872.

6. Paul K. Piff et al., "Awe, the Self, and Prosocial Behavior," *Journal of Personality
   and Social Psychology* 108, no. 6 (2015): 883, www.apa.org/pubs/journals/
   releases/psp-pspi0000018.pdf.

7. W.A. Elwell and P. W. Comfort, in *Tyndale Bible Dictionary* (Carol Stream: IL:
   Tyndale House Publishers, 2001), 618.

8. Isaiah 55:9.

9. Please know that I'm talking here about thought patterns, not about anxiety that
   is rooted in our bodies' chemistry and for which I urge you to seek professional
   help, if that is your situation.

10. Tim Newman, "Anxiety in the West: Is It on the Rise?" *Medical News Today*,
    September 5, 2018, www.medicalnewstoday.com/articles/322877.php.

LEADER'S GUIDE

INTRODUCTION

PHOTO BY: MESHALI MITCHELL

Leaders,

I am excited to partner with you in your efforts to pour into the lives of women! I pray that these few short pages will help to equip and prepare you to lead this study. Many of you may have led plenty of groups in the past, or perhaps this is the first you've led. Whichever the case, this is a spiritual calling and you are entering spiritual places with these women—and spiritual callings and places need spiritual power.

My husband, Zac, always says, "Changed lives change lives." If you are not first aware of your own need for life change, the women around you won't see their need. If you allow God into the inner struggles of your heart, the women following you will be much more likely to let Him into theirs. These women do not need to see bright and shiny, perfectly poised people; they need to see people who are a mess and daily dependent on God for their hope and strength.

The apostle Paul actually believed God and he lived like it. And I think as a generation of women, we are longing for the same lives. We want to have strong minds and thoughts—and to believe God is real and to live like it.

This is not a study for people wanting to keep the status quo. This study messes with you because it shows us how to change our thought patterns and live with freedom from the emotional spirals that suck us down. I want a life like Paul's, who had the mind of Christ. I want to run like he did with a clear, disciplined mind, and ultimately with peace.

Together, we can do this. We can and we will encourage one another, hold each other accountable, and break into each other's spirals to keep our focus individually and collectively on Jesus. That is where we will find true freedom. Minds set free come from minds set on Him. We are not bound by this world and we do have power! Let's take control of our minds and stop the spirals.

Jennie

THE VISION

1. That we would come to realize that the greatest spiritual battle of our generation is being fought between our ears. We have a choice to set our minds on sin and death or life and peace.

We destroy arguments and every lofty opinion raised against the knowledge of God, and take every thought captive to obey Christ (2 Corinthians 10:5).

2. That we would see that God gave us a choice. We can choose to believe the truth of God's Word rather than the lies of the enemy, and we can choose to interrupt the chaos of our minds. We get to choose moment by moment what we live for.

Finally, brothers, whatever is true, whatever is honorable, whatever is just, whatever is pure, whatever is lovely, whatever is commendable, if there is any excellence, if there is any worth of praise, think about these things (Philippians 4:8).

3. That women would believe our focus on Christ changes our behaviors and the more we stop believing lies, the more we will live like Him. The rest of this leader's guide is aimed at equipping you to point the women of your group to God in ways that will change their minds, their thoughts, and ultimately their lives.

> Let this mind be in you which was also in Christ Jesus, who, being in the form of God, did not consider it robbery to be equal with God, but made Himself of no reputation, taking the form of a bondservant, *and* coming in the likeness of men (Philippians 2:5-7 NKJV).

PREPARING YOURSELF TO LEAD A GROUP

1. **Pray:** Pray like the world is ending, pray like this is the last chance for people to know Him, pray like our lives and futures depend on it, pray like the future of souls in heaven is at stake. . . . Pray like you need God.

   Pray for your women:

   ▶ That God would show them the ways they need to get out of their own heads.

   ▶ That they would feel safe to open up and process.

   ▶ That they would want more of God and that God would meet them.

   ▶ That the conversation would be focused on God.

   ▶ That we would be humble displays of God's grace to these women.

   ▶ That God would come and fall on your time together.

   ▶ That many would come to a saving faith as they see God for who He is.

2. **Lean on God:** Allow the Holy Spirit to lead every moment together. We have provided you with tools that we will discuss in the next section; however, they are only tools to use as the Spirit leads you and your time together. God will have unique agendas for each of your groups as you depend on Him. Lean into your own weakness and into His strength and direction.

When Jesus left His disciples to go back to His Father in heaven, He said, "Don't go anywhere until you have the helper I will send you." We need to obey that same command. We don't begin until it is with the power of the Holy Spirit within us (see Acts 1:4–5). He is real and available and waiting to flood our lives and the lives around us as we serve and speak. But we have to wait for Him to speak, ask if we should speak and what we should speak, and ask what to do in different situations. God wants us to need Him and to depend on His Spirit. If this is not how you live on a daily basis, begin today.

3. **Be vulnerable:** If you choose not to be vulnerable, no one else will be vulnerable either. If you desire women to feel safe with you and your group, be vulnerable. This is not an optional assignment. This is your calling as you lead these women.

4. **Listen, but also lead:** Listen as women share struggles. Some women are taking a tremendous risk in being vulnerable with you. Protect them by not interrupting and by instead empathizing. Do not feel the need to speak after each person shares. After most women have shared their answers to a question, turn it back to the Scripture from the study guide, and help them process the truth and hope in their struggles. Avoid lecturing, but do bring the women back to truth.

5. **Model trust:** Show them how you are applying these difficult lessons. Ask God to convict you and lead out with how you are processing change in your own life.

THE STUDY

This study is uniquely designed to work in any venue or location. I envision women leading this in their homes, on campuses, even in their workplaces. Church buildings are the traditional format for group Bible studies and *Get Out of Your Head* will be effective inside the church walls, but the bigger dream is that women would find this study useful in reaching their friends, neighbors, and coworkers.

Whether you find yourself with 150 women in a church auditorium or with a few neighbors in your living room, this study is designed for small groups of women to process truth within their souls. Because of the depth of the questions and topics, it is essential that your group be small enough to share. A maximum of eight women in each group is ideal, preferably fewer. If you are in a larger group, divide into smaller groups with volunteer facilitators. With the help of the leader's guide and the Ask conversation cards, those smaller groups should still prove successful with a little support.

SESSION FORMAT

This six-session study is designed to go deep very quickly. Since women are busy and have full lives, the beauty of this study is it can be led in a living room over a one-hour lunch, or in a church Bible study spread out over two and a half hours. If you have the flexibility, extend the time of sharing in small groups. A frequent complaint is, "We wish we had more time to share." When the group is given deep questions and space to reflect and respond, you'll be surprised how beautiful and plentiful the conversations will be.

These tools are meant to have some flexibility. Here are some suggestions for how to structure your meeting to get the most out of your time together. However, you will be the best judge of what works for your group and the time you have together. Based on your group's needs, choose any combination of going through the questions mixed with reflections from group members' personal study.

HOMEWORK DISCUSSION [10–25 MINUTES]:

After welcoming everyone and opening in prayer, you may choose to begin by having the women discuss their personal reflections as they have worked through the study guide and Scripture in the prior session. If you have more than eight members, break into small groups for this discussion time before reconvening for the video/teaching time.

VIDEO AND/OR TEACHING [15–18 MINUTES]:

Watch the DVD/video to provide a foundation for that session and to help transition to transparent sharing using the Ask conversation cards. If you are supplying teaching in addition to the videos, we recommend you begin with your teaching and then play the video.

ASK CONVERSATION CARDS [30–45 MINUTES]:

Especially if there are more than eight group members, divide into smaller groups and have women go through the Ask conversation cards (instructions on the next page). This will be a time of deep sharing and discussion that is important to learning how to apply all that has been studied that week.

SESSION TOOLS AND HOW TO USE THEM

Study. In the first meeting, distribute your groups' study guides (or if women are purchasing on their own, remind them to bring their study guides to the first meeting). The sessions in the study guide (except for Session One) are meant to be completed during the week before coming to the group meeting. Each session in the guide begins with a short intro before moving into the portion marked Study. The Study portion is followed by four application projects, then closing thoughts from me. The Study portion and projects can be completed in one sitting or broken up into smaller parts throughout the week, depending on each individual woman's needs.

These sessions may feel different from studies you have done in the past. They are very interactive. The goal of the curriculum is to lead women to dig deeply into Scripture and uncover how it applies to their lives, to deeply engage the mind and the heart. Projects, stories, and Bible study all play a role. The projects in the study guide will provide several options for applying Scripture. You and your group members may be drawing or journaling or engaging in some other activity in these projects. At the group meeting discuss your experience in working through the lesson.

See. The teaching videos are meant to set the tone for your time together, to draw women deeper into the Scripture, and to set the stage for transparent sharing. Open each group gathering by reviewing the Study and Projects experiences from the previous week and asking if anyone had anything specific to share or ask about. Watch the short, engaging video teaching to introduce the lesson, set the tone for your time together, and challenge your group to apply Scripture. If your group members want to take notes, encourage them to use the Notes page opposite each SEE title page. Each study guide includes instructions for personal access to streaming video on the inside front cover. This is perfect for anyone who might miss a group gathering, want to rewatch any of the video teaching, or if your group needs to meet on shortened time.

Ask. These cards provide a unique way of starting deep, honest conversations about our thought lives. Each session's cards are labeled with the appropriate session title. These should be pulled out after the video teaching time streaming or DVD.

1. Begin by laying out the Scripture Cards for that specific week.

2. Direct each group member to take a card.

3. Go over the Ground Rules each week. (Ground rules are found on pages 5-6 and on the back of the Instruction card.)

4. Take turns presenting the question on each card to the group. Provide adequate time for everyone in your group to respond to each question.

5. You may only get through a few of the questions. That is fine.

The goals of the questions are to allow women to reflect on what they have studied and heard and have a chance to share their own hearts. Again, allow everyone to concisely and clearly communicate their hearts, but always lead the discussion back to God and what Scripture offers in response that session's topic. Several of the cards each week have Scripture on them to help you do that. Pull one of those if you feel the group needs to hear what God says about the issues.

Lead. This guide serves as a tool to prepare you in leading this study and to encourage you along the way. Refer back to it each prior session to be aware of the goals for each one. The leader's guide will help you effectively point your women to the overarching theme of each session and point them to the themes of the study.

TIPS FOR LEADING YOUR GROUP

The study guide has the following information at the beginning. Review these guidelines carefully. During your first meeting, read through these expectations together as a group. Revisit these guidelines with the group in the coming weeks if necessary.

GET HONEST

This is going to get messy, but it will be worth it. We will be dealing with messy minds. God wants to do something about that. But until we recognize that we are fixing our minds on things other than Him, we will miss what He has for us. If you consider yourself out of control of your thoughts and feelings, perhaps you'll want to change that, even if it is costly. Be honest with yourself and honest with God. He knows all of it already, anyway.

ENGAGE WITH YOUR SMALL GROUP

Do not attempt to deal with such a large thing as the battle for your mind without kindred warriors at your side, fighting with you and for you. Pray, speak truth in love, and hold each other's feet to the fire. Be vulnerable and do not abandon those who are vulnerable with you. Prepare to go to war alongside these women. Keep your group in a safe place to wrestle and discover and also a place filled with truth. John described Christ as being "full of grace and truth" (John 1:14). I pray this is how your small group will also be described.

> And you will know the truth, and the truth will set you free (John 8:32).

Commit to be consistent and present. Every time you gather with your group you will be building your view of God and the way He built the workings of your mind. This study will create a circular understanding of God and His plan, and missing a week will leave a hole in that circle. Every time you are in your small group you will be processing God in your life. Consistency and presence show respect to God and those around you in this process.

Please be quick to listen and slow to speak. Lean into the Holy Spirit as you process together. Speak as He leads. This kind of vulnerable, Spirit-led communication with your group will help lead to lives that are running after the heart of God.

> Let every person be quick to hear, slow to speak (James 1:19).

BE CONCISE. Share your answers to the questions while protecting others' time for sharing. Be thoughtful. Don't be afraid to share with the group, but try not to dominate the conversation.

KEEP GROUP MEMBERS' STORIES CONFIDENTIAL. Many things your group members share are things they are choosing to share with you, not with your husband or other friends. Protect each other by not allowing anything shared in the group to leave the group.

RELY ON SCRIPTURE FOR TRUTH. We are prone to use conventional, worldly wisdom as truth. While there is value in that, this is not the place. If you feel led to respond, please only respond with God's truth and Word, not "advice."

NO COUNSELING. Protect the group by not directing all attention on solving one person's problem. This is the place for confessing and discovery and applying truth together as a group. Your group leader will be able to direct you to more help outside the group time if you need it. Don't be afraid to ask for help.

WHAT *GET OUT OF YOUR HEAD* IS NOT

Sidenote here:

I want to take a moment to acknowledge the truth and reality of mental illness. I've struggled through my own seasons of anxiety and depression and I know. And I'm sorry. I want to say that this study is going to speak of having power over our thoughts and minds, but there are some things we just don't have power over. Chemical imbalances are real and like cancer—you cannot just will yourself to not have cancer. Counseling and medicine can help. If you struggle with mental illness and need help, I encourage you to tell someone, ask, and find the help you need. I also think we all benefit from learning what we do have power over, what weapons we do have, and how we can stop spirals in our minds and take our thoughts captive.

GUIDING CONVERSATION

You may come across some challenges when leading a group conversation. Normally these fall into two categories. In both situations people will need encouragement and grace from you as a leader. As with everything in this study, seek the Holy Spirit's guidance as you interact with your group members.

1. Dominating the conversation: If one woman seems to be dominating the conversation or going into detail that makes the rest of the group uncomfortable, gently interrupt her if necessary and thank her for sharing. Avoid embarrassing her in front of the group. Ask if there is anyone else who would like to share in response to the original question

asked (not to necessarily respond to the woman who was just speaking). If the problem persists, talk with the woman outside of the group time. Affirm her for her vulnerability and willingness to share, and be prepared to refer her for more help if the need arises.

2. Not sharing as much as the others: If you notice there is a woman who seems to not be as talkative as the others in the group, you may try gently asking for her input directly at some point in the conversation. Some women are naturally shyer than others; don't try to force them into an extroverted role, but do let them know their input is valuable to the group. Remind them of the goals of the study and how being vulnerable with one another is one of the ways God shapes us spiritually. If a woman is just not interested in being in the study and is holding the rest of the group back, meet with her outside the group setting to discuss her further involvement.

Keep in mind that no two women are alike, but keep the best interests of the group in mind as you lead. For more information on two kinds of learners, see page 22.

WHEN TO REFER

Some of the women in your care may be suffering past the point you feel able to help. This study may bring the pain of adverse thoughts and emotions to the surface. To leave women in this state would be more damaging than helpful. Don't try to take on problems you do not feel equipped to handle. If you sense that a woman may need more help, follow up and refer her to someone.

Check with your church or pastor for names of trusted, certified Christian counselors. Some major indicators of this need would be: depression, anxiety, suicide, abuse, broken marriage. These are the obvious ones, but honestly, some women who are stuck in hurt from their past, minor depression, or fear could also benefit from counseling. I believe counseling is beneficial for many. So keep a stash of names for anyone you may feel needs to process further with a professional.

▶ Look for the nearest Celebrate Recovery group and offer to attend the first meeting with her (www.celebraterecovery.com).

▶ Suggest further resources and help to make a plan for their future growth and well-being.

▶ Communicate with the leadership at your church about how to proceed with care.

▶ Do not abandon these hurting women in a vulnerable place. This may be the first time they have opened up about painful hurts or patterns. Own their care and see it through. If they have landed in your group, God has assigned them to you for this season, until they are trusted to the care of someone else. Even then, continue to check in on them.

TYPES OF LEARNERS

Hopefully, you will be blessed to be leading this study with a group diverse in age, experience, and style. While the benefits of coming together as a diverse group to discuss God outweigh the challenges by a mile, there are often distinctions in learning styles. Just be aware and consider some of the differences in two types of learning styles that may be represented. (These are obviously generalizations, and each woman as an individual will express her own unique communication style, but in general these are common characteristics.)

EXPERIENTIAL LEARNERS

There are women who are more transparent, don't like anything cheesy, want to go deep quickly, and are passionate. Make a safe environment for them by being transparent yourself and engaging their hearts. These women may not care as much about head knowledge and may care more deeply how knowledge about God applies to their lives. They want to avoid being put in a box. Keep the focus on applying truth to their lives and they will stay engaged. Don't preach to them; be real and show them through your experiences how to pursue the mind of Christ.

PRAGMATIC LEARNERS

These women are more accustomed to a traditional, inductive, or precept approach to Bible study. They have a high value for truth and authority but may not place as high a value on the emotional aspects of confessing sin and being vulnerable. To them it may feel unnecessary or dramatic. Keep the focus on the truth of Scripture. These women keep truth in the forefront of their lives and play a valuable role in discipleship.

***

Because this study is different from traditional studies, some women may need more time to get used to the approach of this study. The goal is still to make God big in our lives, to fix our minds on Him, and to choose where to train our thoughts. We all just approach it in unique ways to reach unique types of people. I actually wrote this study praying it could reach both types of learners. I am one who lives with a foot in both worlds, trying to apply the deep truths I gained in seminary in an experiential way. I pray that this study would deeply engage the heart and the mind, and that we would be people who worship God in spirit and in truth, not just learning about the battle for our minds but going to war for them together.

Common struggles like fear, stress, anger, shame, and insecurity are not respecters of age, religion, or income level. These struggles are human, and I have seen this study transcend the typical boundaries of Christian and seeker, young and old, single and married, needy and comfortable, bringing these women together and to God in a unique and powerful way.

In the following pages and notes for each session, I hope I have given you enough guidance that you do not feel lost, but enough freedom to depend on the Holy Spirit. These are only suggestions, but hopefully these notes will help surface themes and goals to guide you through your discussion of group members' homework and through the discussion of the Ask conversation cards. The video, homework, and cards should provide more than enough material for great discussions, but stay on track and be sure people are walking away with hope and truth.

SPIRALING OUT

OPEN

SPIRALING OUT

When we pay attention to what's going on in our heads, we realize we have a choice.

During this first meeting you will be getting to know each other, handing out the study guides, walking through the Instructions and Expectations (found on pp. 4–7 of the study guide), and watching the first video.

Here are some general goals and thoughts for your time together this week:

▶ Make the women feel safe.

▶ Get to know each other and the things you each struggle with.

▶ Set expectations for the study.

▶ Instruct group members on how to use the study guide, where to take notes from the video, and how you will use the Ask conversation cards.

▶ Create a need for this study in their lives by helping them see that we all are in a battle for our minds.

▶ Remind them that God is longing for a real relationship with each of us.

▶ Introduce the book of Philippians.

LEADER: This first session's suggested format is different from the others since it is your first meeting and there is no homework to review.

SEE—VIDEO TEACHING

For this first meeting, it is best to begin by watching the video session "INTRODUCTION: SPIRALING OUT." Remind women they can take notes from the teaching in their study guide to reference later in discussion or homework.

ASK—GROUP DISCUSSION TIME

1. Together take some time to read the Introduction, Instructions and Expectations, and the first session in the study guide either aloud or to yourselves and discuss.

2. When you reach page 25 in the first session of the study guide, have participants choose the ten things their minds are trained on most. Give everyone time to think about this, write down their answers in their guides, and fill out their mind maps.

3. If you are in a large group, break into small groups and give each person the chance to open up about their maps. Leaders, share first and be transparent.

4. After all the women have shared, you may transition to the Ask conversation cards to continue your discussion. The cards for this session are labeled "INTRODUCTION: SPIRALING OUT" on the front. Distribute the Ask cards and guide the women to ask and answer the questions on the cards. Review the Ask card instructions together. Remember to begin with the Scripture card and end by stressing the scriptural truth group members can apply to their lives as a result

of what they discussed in your group time. Close this discussion by praying for your coming weeks together and praising God for His Word and His unwavering love and pursuit of us.

I have seen everything that is done under the sun, and behold, all is vanity and a striving after wind (Ecclesiastes 1:14).

Instruct the group to complete Session 2: MAKE THE SHIFT Study and Projects before the next group meeting.

MAKE THE SHIFT

MAIN IDEA

The mind of Christ is available to us—we just have to choose the direction of our thoughts.

In this session we will look at how we interrupt the spirals in our minds by making the shift up, toward God. We all have things we fixate on, and they can become idols if we make them our main focus. Paul cultivated the "mind of Christ" by making God the only and main thing. This is the starting point of our work and the only way it sticks. We have a choice to stop our spiraling thoughts, but we have to make the bigger choice first to point ourselves toward Him.

Here are some general goals and thoughts for your time together this week:

▶ Identify and define some of the things we fixate on to make us happy.

▶ Discover how Paul's calling was similar to God's calling for us.

▶ Discuss the things God says about who He is.

▶ A strong mind comes from surrender to God; we are not subject to our own thoughts and feelings but can make a choice to continually turn toward Him.

MAIN GOAL

Lead people to an honest evaluation of the source of their fixations, and encourage them to set their mind on the spirit.

OPEN—HOMEWORK DISCUSSION

Suggestions on places to focus as you go over the homework with your group:

▶ Ask the group to share what they learned as they studied Paul in Philippians 1.

▶ Ask how Romans 8:5–11 speaks to them now in their lives.

▶ Discuss their response to Project 2.

▶ Ask what else they learned as they studied and interacted with the session and Scripture this week.

SEE—VIDEO TEACHING

Watch the video session "MAKE THE SHIFT." Remind women they can take notes from the teaching in their study guide to reference later in discussion or homework.

ASK—GROUP DISCUSSION TIME

If you are in a large group, break into small groups for discussion time using the Ask conversation cards. Distribute this session's Ask cards and guide the women to ask and answer the questions on the cards. Remember to begin with the Scripture card and end by stressing the scriptural truth group members can apply to their lives as a result of what you discussed in your group time. Close this discussion by praying for the things shared and praising God for His position in our lives and in eternity.

> "For who has understood the mind of the Lord so as to instruct him?"
> But we have the mind of Christ (1 Corinthians 2:16).

Instruct the group to complete Session 3: WEAPONS WE USE, PART 1 Study and Projects before the next group meeting.

NOTES

_____

_____

_____

_____

_____

_____

_____

_____

_____

_____

_____

_____

_____

SESSION 3

WEAPONS WE USE

PART 1

MAIN IDEA

As we are developing the mind of Christ, we'll have a fight on our hands. But God gives us a weapon for every attack of the enemy.

Here are some general goals and thoughts for your time together this week:

▶ Create awareness of the way our inputs affect our attitudes.

▶ Create a dissatisfaction with the things the world throws at us to keep us distracted, like self-absorption, noise, and cynicism.

▶ What does it look like to live with humility? To be strengthened by silence? To welcome delight?

▶ The battle for the future is being fought between our ears; we participate in the renewal of our minds by filling them with the truth.

MAIN GOAL

Energize people to fight for their minds, encouraging them that renewal happens as we make choices for things of God rather than the distractions of the world.

OPEN—HOMEWORK DISCUSSION

Suggestions on places to focus as you go over the homework with your group:

▶ Discuss their readings of Philippians 2.

▶ Which of the three spirals is most common for you?

▶ What was God speaking to you through Romans 12:1–2?

▶ Have women share their drawings from Project 2.

▶ Ask what else they learned as they studied and interacted with the lesson and Scripture this week.

SEE—VIDEO TEACHING

Watch the video session "WEAPONS WE USE, PART 1." Remind women they can take notes from the teaching in their study guide to reference later in discussion or homework.

ASK—GROUP DISCUSSION TIME

If you are in a large group, break into small groups for discussion time using the Ask conversation cards. Distribute this session's Ask cards and guide the women to ask and answer the questions on the cards. Remember to begin with the Scripture card and end by stressing the scriptural truth group members can apply to their lives as a result of what they discussed in your group time. Close this discussion by praying for the things shared and praising God for His position in our lives and in eternity.

> To the Jews who had believed him, Jesus said, "If you hold to my teaching, you are really my disciples. Then you will know the truth, and the truth will set you free" (John 8:31–32 NIV).

Instruct the group to complete Session 4: WEAPONS WE USE, PART 2 Study and Projects before the next group meeting.

SESSION 4

WEAPONS WE USE

PART 2

MAIN IDEA

Our comfort zones can be dangerous places to dwell; God urges us out of them, toward connection, intentionality, and gratefulness.

Here are some general goals and thoughts for your time together this session:

▶ Help women to see that there are better options than victim mentality, complacency, and isolation.

▶ If we know God and trust Him we will obey no matter the cost, even if it feels uncomfortable.

▶ Every small shift toward service and connection makes a big impact on our minds.

▶ We weren't meant to be alone in the dark. God wants so much more for us, and for those He's put in our paths.

MAIN GOAL

Lead people to a right understanding of the gifts God gives us in community, in service, in gratefulness as they fight their spirals.

OPEN—HOMEWORK DISCUSSION

Suggestions on places to focus as you go over the homework with your group:

What were the differences between Paul's approach to hardship and what we'd typically hear today?

▶ What did you feel as you reread Philippians 2?

▶ Which project stood out to you most this session?

▶ Ask what else they learned as they studied and interacted with the session and Scripture this week.

SEE—VIDEO TEACHING

Watch the video session "WEAPONS WE USE, PART 2." Remind women they can take notes from the teaching in their study guide to reference later in discussion or homework.

ASK—GROUP DISCUSSION TIME

If you are in a large group, break into small groups for discussion time using the Ask conversation cards. Distribute this session's Ask cards and guide the women to ask and answer the questions on the cards. Remember to begin with the Scripture card and end by stressing the scriptural truth group members can apply to their lives as a result of what they discussed in your group time. Close this discussion by praying for the things shared and praising God for His position in our lives and in eternity.

> Keep your heart with all vigilance, for from it flow the springs of life (Proverbs 4:23).

Instruct the group to complete Session 5: A NEW WAY TO LIVE Study and Projects before the next group meeting.

A NEW WAY TO LIVE

MAIN IDEA

As we develop the mind of Christ, we're growing in maturity. Once we leave our spirals and our past behind, we replace them with what we're running toward and growing into.

Here are some general goals and thoughts for your time together this session:

▶ Explain the concept of maturity according to Paul in Philippians 3.

▶ As someone with the mind of Christ, you'll never be at home in the darkness again. Forget what is behind and press on toward what is ahead for you.

▶ Once we've dumped the bondage, we have to replace it with something.

▶ Focus on the running, and our hindrances will fall off *as we run.*

▶ Freed people free people—we're a new creation with a job to do!

▶ We ask God for more faith. We go to Him with our doubts.

MAIN GOAL

Lead people to address the bondage of their past, bring it to God, and walk forward in maturity.

OPEN—HOMEWORK DISCUSSION

Suggestions on places to focus as you go over the homework with your group:

▶ Talk about Paul's approach to "forgetting." Where did it come from?

▶ Discuss how that attitude would transform our lives today.

▶ Share your summaries of Philippians 3. What stood out most?

▶ Discuss the patterns in Project 3. Where do your women most desire to mature?

▶ Ask what else they learned as they studied and interacted with the session and Scripture this week.

SEE—VIDEO TEACHING

Watch the video session "A NEW WAY TO LIVE." Remind women they can take notes from the teaching in their study guide to reference later in discussion or homework.

ASK—GROUP DISCUSSION TIME

If you are in a large group, break into small groups for discussion time using the Ask conversation cards. Distribute this session's Ask cards and guide the women to ask and answer the questions on the cards. Remember to begin with the Scripture card and end by stressing the scriptural truth group members can apply to their lives as a result of what they discussed in your group time. Close this discussion by praying for the things shared and praising God for His position in our lives and in eternity.

Indeed, I count everything as loss because of the surpassing worth of knowing Christ Jesus my Lord. For his sake I have suffered the loss of all things and count them as rubbish, in order that I may gain Christ and be found in him, not having a righteousness of my own that comes from the law, but that which comes through faith in Christ, the righteousness from God that depends on faith (Philippians 3:8-9).

Instruct the group to complete Session 6: A MIND LIKE CHRIST Study and Projects before the next group meeting.

NOTES

SESSION 6

A MIND LIKE CHRIST

MAIN IDEA

The mind of Christ focuses on whatever is true, freed from lies and anxieties.

Here are some general goals and thoughts for your time together this session:

▶ Developing the mind of Christ is the project of a lifetime, but don't give up.

▶ God is with you in this war, as we learn to "think on these things."

▶ The lies we believe fall into three categories, but God gives us fundamental truths that will continue to set you free as you battle on into the future.

▶ Contentment is a result of a healthy mind. Walking with Jesus is the only thing that satisfies.

MAIN GOAL

Encourage people to keep fighting, to be honest about the lies they believe, and to hold fiercely to the truths God gives us.

OPEN—HOMEWORK DISCUSSION

Suggestions on places to focus as you go over the homework with your group:

▶ What did you think of Paul's instruction to not be anxious about anything? How does that hit you?

▶ Discuss Paul's secret to contentment. How does this power us through our every day?

▶ Have women share their grids from Project 1.

▶ What are your reactions to 2 Corinthians 2:11–16?

▶ Ask what else they learned as they studied and interacted with the session and Scripture this week.

SEE—VIDEO TEACHING

Watch the video "A MIND LIKE CHRIST." Remind women they can take notes from the teaching in their study guide to reference later in discussion or homework.

ASK—GROUP DISCUSSION TIME

If you are in a large group, break into small groups for discussion time using the Ask conversation cards. Distribute this session's Ask cards and guide the women to ask and answer the questions on the cards. Remember to begin with the Scripture card and end by stressing the scriptural truth group members can apply to their lives as a result of what they discussed in your group time. Close this discussion by praying for the things shared and praising God for His position in our lives and in eternity.

Finally, brothers, whatever is true, whatever is honorable, whatever is just, whatever is pure, whatever is lovely, whatever is commendable, if there is any excellence, if there is anything worthy of praise, think about these things. What you have learned and received and heard and seen in me—practice these things, and the God of peace will be with you (Philippians 4:8–9).

NOTES

You are in charge of your thoughts.
They are not in charge of you.

Get Out of Your Head: Stopping the Spiral of Toxic Thoughts is a Biblical guide to discovering how to submit our minds to Christ because how we think shapes how we live. As we surrender every thought to Jesus, the promises of God flood our lives in profound ways.

Visit **getoutofyourheadbook.com** for info about **Get Out of Your Head.**

Available wherever books are sold.

ALSO AVAILABLE FROM JENNIE ALLEN

BUILDING DEEP COMMUNITY IN A LONELY WORLD

This seven-session video Bible study looks at the original community in Genesis and the Trinity to see how God intended for us to live in community all along.

IDENTIFY THE THREADS OF YOUR LIFE

Stuck is an eight-session video Bible study leading women through the invisible struggles that we fight and to the God who has to set us free.

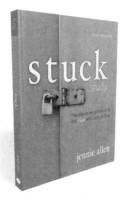

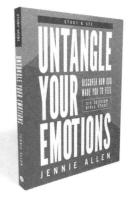

IDENTIFY THE THREADS OF YOUR LIFE

In this eight-session video Bible study using the story of Joseph, Jennie explains how his suffering, gifts, story, and relationships fit into the greater story of God—and how your story can do the same.

WHAT THE BIBLE TELLS US ABOUT OUR EMOTIONS

This six-session video Bible study teaches how your emotions actually help you notice what's wrong and connect with God and others more deeply.

YOU ARE ENOUGH BECAUSE JESUS IS ENOUGH.

In this eight-session video Bible study, Jennie Allen walks through key passages in the Gospel of John that demonstrate how Jesus is enough. We don't have to prove anything because Jesus has proven everything.

CHASING AFTER THE HEART OF GOD

Chase is an eight-session video Bible study experience to discover the heart of God and what it is exactly He wants from us through major events in the life of David and the Psalms.

Visit JennieAllen.com for more info. Available wherever books & Bibles are sold.

We Aren't Supposed to Be This Lonely.

But you don't have to stay there. Let's find your people.

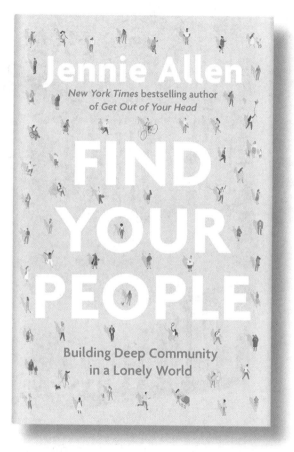

You were created to play, engage, adventure, and explore—with others. In *Find Your People*, you'll discover exactly how to dive into the deep end and experience the full wonder of community. Because while the ache of loneliness is real, it doesn't have to be your reality.

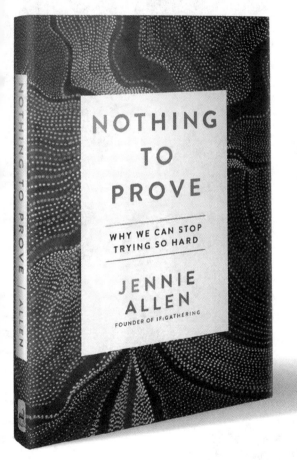